T0352821

High-rise buildings as objects of financial investments have an immediate impact on the built environment. Buildings have become assets and air rights have developed into a speculative commodity. Manhattan, with its long history of converting incoming capital to high density building mass, has been at the forefront of development and therefore seems to be uniquely equipped as a location to examine the phenomena of speculation, asset architecture, and its effects.

ALI RAHIM

Professor of Architecture and Director, MSD-Advanced Architectural Design

No.3

TABLE OF CONTENTS

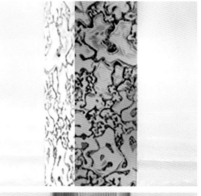

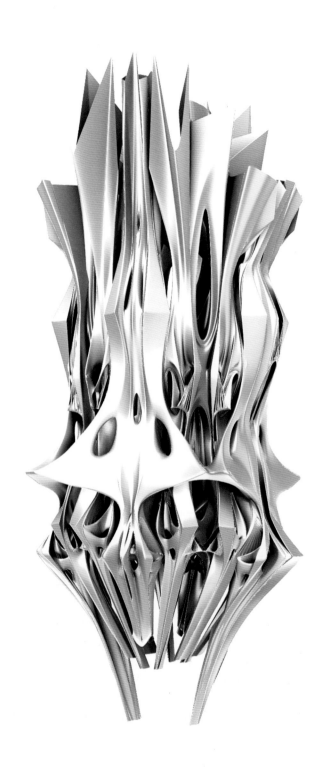

ALI RAHIM

ASSET ARCHITECTURE

Asset Architecture 3 brought to the fore why design architects today need to be technologically focused due to the many competing pressures within the discipline.

Innovation is the introduction of something new and is synonymous with difference and advancement. As one does not generally innovate backwards in time, innovation is oriented toward the future, but is grounded in the present. Innovation proposes to take us from here to there. Architects are accustomed to thinking about themselves as innovators and architectural innovation is accelerated by technology, especially the digital technology we have available to us today. Technology is a powerful and transformative entity because it bridges between the sciences and culture, constructing links between knowledge and production. Examples from the history of architecture, the arts, the sciences, and media all point to technology as a powerful influence on culture and its effects are some of the most important aspects of cultural endeavors.[1]

What does this mean for practitioners of architecture today? We are certainly aware of architecture's relationship to other disciplines and to larger industries that are generally resistant to change. Where do architects and other designers who are interested in initiating change and innovation direct their efforts? How does one evaluate the success or usefulness of such change? We cannot begin to answer these questions in a vacuum. We need feedback. Feedback is a fundamentally simple concept: information goes out, perhaps in the form of actions, and information returns to inform future action. It is a two-way transfer of information. Feedback plays a prominent role in innovation, and is a vehicle for the development or advancement of any innovation. It is also the means by which the usefulness of an innovation may be evaluated and is a subject to which we will return throughout this book because most importantly, it is necessary for the development of techniques.

Why the distinction between technique and technology? Technique is already embedded within culture and operates as part of a complex system between technologies and their context. When it comes to encouraging cultural change and innovation, technology is not enough. Techniques are crucial not only to harness the powerful potential of new technologies and direct that potential towards influencing cultural development. New technologies require techniques in order to fulfill their potential and likewise, new or more advanced techniques often have the effect of bringing advancements from different lineages together in order to stimulate technological development.

Why the distinction between technology and the technical? Technological development anticipates and responds to cultural change in a continuous condition of feedback, unlike purely technical tinkering and refinement, which is void of meaning outside formal and functional efficiency of its mechanical operation with its own logics and laws. The technical is reduced to a numerical abstraction measured by a quantity that bears a direct correspondence to its behavior, which is efficient and tends to be singularly focused on particular mechanical operations. The technical threshold is only crossed when it becomes useful and is located in a context. Any assessment of technological effectiveness is fundamentally the interaction between technology and the user producing a pattern of behaviors that can result in new levels of performance and newly effective behaviors and actions. It is qualitative as is cultural efficacy and its effects are greater than the sum of its parts. Technology is crucial not only to make the technical useful, but is pivotal to the development of techniques and innovation.

Techniques are important because they are fundamentally innovative methods for action and change. They are the intelligence required to locate oneself and operate within a particular context and are developed through cognition and involve the use of tools, artifacts, and concepts that are external to users. Techniques are behaviors and procedures that are systematic, repeatable, and communicable. They often must be developed for the purpose of accomplishing new tasks that are complex or difficult. Feedback plays a significant role. Over time, when existing techniques no longer adequately address solutions to

problems, new techniques must be developed through experimentation.

For example, in aerial warfare, techniques are learned through training and flying experience and developed through use. If a pilot is engaged in combat, the technology of the airplane is reliant on techniques to maneuver out of harms way. The techniques enable pilots to fly their planes in particular ways such as tight or loose to avoid harm. With time, enemy pilots develop techniques to counter techniques being used against them. Hence, new techniques to out maneuver the enemy have to be continually developed. As this negotiation unfolds, pressure is placed on the government by the military to develop technical research to develop higher performing planes. As the technical engine is invented, it requires a new chasse that is capable of resisting the power of the new engine, which pressures new materials to be developed that are strong and lightweight enough to take flight. As the new technology of the plane is released to the military, pilots are re-trained and develop new techniques to fly. At the same time, others develop newer airplanes as well to maintain control of the skies. New techniques develop to counter techniques being developed by other nation states, and this pressures further technical development.

As technologies are based on application, they only exist within cultural contexts. New technologies require the invention of new techniques in order for them to be effective. Techniques are pervasive throughout culture, affecting new behaviors and producing new subjects of knowledge. Therefore, techniques also proliferate within culture, establishing new goals and new technological horizons. Not only do they provide the means for people to interact with technology, they are insistent with respect to its development and acceleration.

Innovation is only possible when there is a fluency with techniques, and basic techniques are usually required in order for more innovative ones to be invented. A model for architecture that seeks to participate in a process of cultural change would demand that architecture develop with technology. This is a model for design that is capable of consistently transforming and progressing, keeping pace with cultural change all through the development of nimble and flexible techniques.

For instance, when new techniques have been incorporated into architecture, they have the effect of enabling new methods and forms of building. Techniques influence the design of objects, which in turn produce effects that influence human behaviors. Techniques are also understood as behaviors that arise through putting technology in motion within culture. For our purposes, technology is understood to be the application of scientific advances in a particular cultural context. It is thus often linked to the idea of science without a pure or strictly controlled environment, possessing no specific doctrine of its own, but consisting of different applications of the advances made in science. Technology in this sense is not an efficiency-oriented practice, measured by quantities, but a qualitative set of relations that interact with cultural stimuli, resulting in behaviors, some of which are techniques.

The path of development produced by any entity – an object, a building, a company, or a career immersed in its context – produces a distinct lineage as a result of its progression. Internal pressures drive each lineage and external pressures determine its usefulness. Although different lineages are separate, they inevitably emanate and influence each other. This is a process in which many conditions may be interrelated through complex feedback loops. This interrelation is innovative and cognitive, leading to a restless proliferation of new effects. The development of techniques applied to a particular discipline, such as architecture may constitute its own lineage, but

techniques are notable because they bring together advancements from other lineages as well. This transmission across lineages is the major source of cultural change.[2]

The discipline of architecture relies upon the crossing of numerous disciplines: material sciences, natural sciences, mathematics, physics, the visual arts, and philosophy. These are affiliated with patterns of settlement, commerce, social interaction, and culture, which all intermingle, transmitting knowledge from one to another. Disciplines must be open to change. Architecture has always incorporated knowledge and innovation from its practitioners and from other fields.

For the purposes of *Asset Architecture 3*, techniques are characterized by four principal characteristics. First, techniques incorporate feedback. Feedback is a prerequisite for techniques and always generate results that inform their future behavior and development. Over the course of this development, many techniques simply become automatic and are absorbed relatively seamlessly by users. Those users become one with the technology. Driving an automobile, for instance is a collection of individual techniques, many of which become automatic through repetition and familiarity. This underscores the second characteristic, that new techniques are destabilizing elements. They exist to produce change and work against equilibrium and stasis because they begin to reinvent standard practices. Third, techniques are process-driven. They often proceed from trial and error and work over time, adjusted over the course of their development until new techniques are required. Fourth, techniques are interrelational. They work across different disciplines, encouraging and facilitating the transmission of advancements and expertise across disciplinary boundaries in order to generate change.

We use techniques to produce new and different effects in culture and that are transformative within cultures, providing the means for users to develop and implement new technological applications. As technologies develop and become more complex and effective, they incorporate parallel uses and different lineages in an effort to remain useful. For precisely this reason, the personal computer is now a calculator, a communications device, a word processor, an editor of photographs and a machine for playing music or watching a film. Each individual function is an indication of greater capacity for usefulness and made possible through the many redundant circuits and devices incorporated within the computer. Techniques have the effect of demanding greater redundancy within technology through an insistence on development as a means towards greater technological effectiveness in the short and long term.

Technological effectiveness is provided with flexibility. The usefulness of a personal computer is based in part on its ability to be useful in many different ways. Its flexibility means that it will continue to be used differently depending upon its user or application and that the same device is useful in a variety of situations. The danger with techniques and technology is always that they will become routine and static through their use, no longer capable of or inclined toward innovation. Techniques and even some technologies that might have previously had the effect of encouraging change and innovation become purely technical. For instance, tools such as computer-aided-drafting (CAD) and processes such as computer aided design and manufacturing (CAD/CAM) have become widely available to large practices and individual practitioners alike. These tools harness the powerful capability of digital computing, but are kept discretely separate from architectural innovation. Digital tools such as design software are used widely within architectural practices as tools for documenting or visualization tools for translating formal ideas into construction documents or fabrication. These tools are technical because they are applied to architectural

practice in mechanical or automatic ways the way previous generations of architects employed technical pens and parallel rulers. Their capacity to influence and affect the way that architects think and operate is causal and limited. There is no relation between architectural design, construction methods and the use of techniques, which is clearly illustrated by most corporate offices where younger architects implement an idea that has been developed without the use of techniques. CAD is applied in order to make this task more efficient and CAD software's refinement over time is driven toward solidifying this position so it acquires an increasingly static and technical role within architectural practice. This arrangement relies on a collaged process that simply superimposes and overlays technology to design, instead of constructing adaptable working methods that move beyond using digital technology for efficiency of execution.

The disciplines and devices that are referred to as being technical are largely oriented towards efficiency. Technical devices are mechanical and highly specialized for specific tasks and for specific applications. For this reason, technical advances are generally isolated from larger contexts. This isolation is a necessary feature of technical disciplines, ensuring precision and control. It is also evident in the emphasis within technical disciplines on efficiency. Performance in a technical context refers only to an object or device's function in its own lineage as if in a vacuum, separated from context or any other factors that exist outside of the technical lineage. Notions of performance within technical settings are quantitative rather than qualitative and seek greater efficiency through the accomplishing of tasks with less material, fewer parts and less resistance.

Technical devices are therefore referred to by their function, for example levels, switches, sorters, tabulators and processors to name a few. Technical refinement is also generally constrained by these

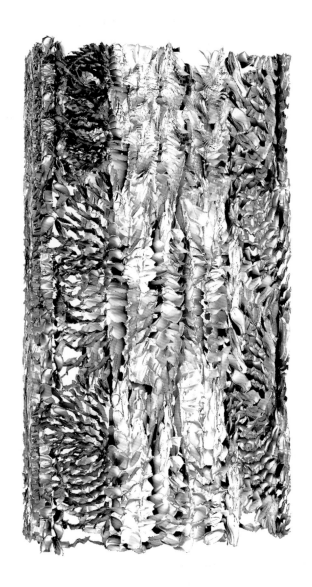

FACADE MODEL: STORAGE TOWER - LIANGQI SONG, YUNZHONGDA PENG, KYUHUN KIM

functions and characterized by greater efficiency. The difference between a 2000-megahertz processor and a 3000-megahertz processor is a factor of this efficiency. The higher performance processor is superior to the lesser chip because it is faster, but greater processing speed only matters when it begins to make particular computational applications possible. When it transforms to becoming a technology, it shifts from efficiency to effectiveness. Purely technical advancement is not an end unto itself. This obsession with efficiency is prevalent throughout society and reflected in the design of many devices and systems, but it has not demonstrated an understanding of technology, as it has existed historically, as it exists today, and as it may exist in the future. The technical therefore is unlikely to produce new effects in cultural efficacy.

Technical tools and devices alone are constantly threatened with extinction due to their inability to adapt to or affect cultural change. Implements and tools exist because of specific local needs. Their refinement and development is guided by their local necessities, and as the pressures from their necessities change, in order to survive, so do the tools. The most obvious pressure is war. The government funds the military, which funds industries to drive technical advances that prove beneficial to the winning of a war. This puts emphasis on either one lineage, or puts pressures on several industries to collaborate to cross lineages and produce new technical innovations. After these innovations have developed into the technical, then they still need to be used, to escape extinction by being immersed in their context. If a new technical device or discovery does not find an immediate use it may exist until a future time when it becomes necessary. Hence, advancement in tools can serve as a catalyst for change in a particular context. If this does not occur, then the tools themselves are threatened with extinction.

Technical discoveries that lay dormant may be resurrected later in time becoming part of technology. Certain technologies may exist indefinitely through time, essentially unchanged until they are recognized and put to use within technological developments that occur much later in time.[3] For example, mathematical tables were developed by Charles Babbage in 1819 and first were used to assist in calculations that had become necessary for naval navigation as England's empire expanded. Mathematical tables were also used for the process of industrialization, which created a demand to assist in accounting calculations and actuarial purposes. Babbage introduced a control element in the form of punched cards. This crossed the lineage of the mechanical loom that was invented by Joseph-Marie Jacquard in1804. The punch card driven loom was revolutionary because patterns could be stored on cards and reused, effectively eliminating tedious time-consuming setups. Babbages' machine automated the mental processes of mathematics to perform calculations that were essential to an empire that was creating more information than could be handled by humans alone. This invention was never successfully built. However, the ideas of this technical lineage became relevant later, due to two external pressures from the United States, first from the need to organize and coordinate times for train schedules brought on by a devastating train crash from Albany to Worcester in 1841, and the need to quickly organize and tabulate information of a growing population for the Census Bureau which had taken eight years to tabulate and process in 1880. Herman Hollerith designed a new technical device based on a punch card system. Information could be stored on cards with standardized perforations and read on a machine. With the machine, the Census Bureau could determine every possible combination of data with little extra effort. Here the technical invention of Babbage of the punched card was re-activated and became useful in Hollerith's invention. If these two pressures did not exist, the technical invention would have become extinct and lost. Using Hollerith's system, the population count from the 1890 census returns was completed within six[4] weeks. Later, in 1911, Hollerith's company – the Tabulating Machine Company merged with two other companies to create the Computing-Tabulating-Recording Company, which was renamed International Business Machines (IBM) in 1924. Here technology absorbed the technical invention of the punch card at a later time, incorporating technical tools, methods and devices that different lineages had developed. The government, an external pressure, funded a competition to accelerate the invention of the punch card which crossed lineages to produce a new technical innovation. After this process, the technical is still needed to be used by culture to escape extinction. If a new technical device or discovery created by tinkering does not find immediate use it may exist until a future time when it becomes necessary.

Punch cards once again became crucial to another lineage for complex scientific calculations in the 1930s. By 1937, Howard Aiken had developed an automatic sequence-controlled calculator that made the storing and retrieving of data automatic, using punched tapes and electrical and mechanical parts. The Harvard Mark 1 as it was called was used for naval weapons design and for generating complex ballistic firing tables.

The ENIAC, developed at the University of Pennsylvania beginning in 1941 was also born out of speed and conflict and was used for thermonuclear bomb calculations. Early computers such as the ENIAC were application-specific at any one time. Instructions were entered directly into it by literally rewiring its circuitry and setting switches, fixing the computer's hardware into a configuration that would solve a particular problem. Vacuum tubes and later, transistors made this type of early programming obsolete, resulting in techniques for simple binary programming that would instruct the computer directly. Subsequent development brought assembly language, which crossed the technical threshold between absolute addressing with 1s and 0s and machine language where written commands would be translated into instructions for the computer by directing the computer to an area of memory where the actual instructions were stored. The first real programming languages were assemblages of these simple machine languages. These rudimentary programming languages operated technologically, prompting computer users to develop new techniques for scripting code from them. As more discrete instruction sets began to be standardized, they were formulated into subroutines that could be reused for different programs. This was the beginning of the formal concept of software that would serve as a mediating technology between human beings and computers.

The development of digital technology and media themselves make evident the relations between scientific, artistic and technological advancement that is a feature of technological practices. The development and use of the computer also offers a clear example of the feedback between the technical, the technological, and technique and the effects that are produced as a result. The computer is a particularly transformative technology. It has the potential to affect its users who must develop new techniques in order to access its capacity. It also embodies a crossing of many technical lineages and devices and as such, the actual personal computer is also an effect of the crossing of technical thresholds, the pressures that drove that refinement, and the techniques that were developed in order to advance its development. Such is the complex nature of this system of relations.

The personal computer brings together many different lineages, and housed within the computer are a variety of individual devices such as relays, tabulators, processors, each with its own lineage of development, and brought together through a variety of different technological, economic, military, and academic pressures. These devices are not earlier versions of the computer. A calculator is not a primitive computer, though they share a common ancestry. The development of technology over time is therefore not evolutionary in a precise sense. Technological development over time is occasionally mapped as an evolutionary tree, with each device producing more branches of slightly more refined devices that have a more specific function. A more accurate representation of this development would look more like a dense forest with intertwining among branches so intense as to make a direct tracing back to simpler ancestors difficult. Technological development does produce different devices like a computer and a calculator, but these different lineages are not the result of simple branching.

By 1964 political pressure in the form of Lyndon Johnson's *Great Society* created vast demand for record keeping, establishing new technical horizons for computer memory. Likewise, the 1961 challenge to put a man on the Moon had transformed the American space program into a massive complex of technical institutions with enormous budgets and vast demands for computing power.[5] Though initially military in origin, techniques to access this computational potential were developed by users in the private business sector as well, prompting IBM's entry into the digital computer market in 1952 with its introduction of a lineage of dedicated business computing machines that would develop parallel to those being developed for scientific and governmental purposes. The separation of computer development into two separate technical lineages gave way to separate programming disciplines dedicated to producing software for each type of machine and each user application which were not brought back together within the discipline of computer science until after the advent of the System/360 in 1964.

The computer is not descended from a loom and the magnetic and optical computer memory that we use now is not related in any direct or evolutionary sense to Jacquard's punched paper card. Nevertheless, they may be thought of as being part of the same technological development, having been brought together well after the innovation of the punch card itself. But despite the fact that the card was no longer itself an innovative invention, once recontextualized as a memory device within a new and different lineage, it continued to support and initiate further innovations and new techniques until a technical threshold was reached and a new technical horizon identified with magnetic memory, which was followed by optical memory, and so on. Many technical innovations and mechanisms have to wait until other lineages or technological development and culture as a whole have progressed to a point where they can be useful.[6] For this reason, it is difficult to anticipate future technical arrangements because purely technical development ignores all other factors and follows an autonomous process, oriented towards achieving greater efficiency. Many technical discoveries simply lie dormant until they can be brought forward in time with the recognition that they are capable of playing a vital role in contemporary technical assemblages.[7]

As techniques, new technologies always have the potential to radically transform existing design practices. In order to counter the drive toward stasis and technical efficiency, techniques for design that are sufficiently flexible and interrelational are necessary. Innovation and its impact on cultural and technological development are only possible with techniques that proceed from the standpoint of bringing together advances and knowledge from as many different sources and in as many applications as possible. Such techniques serve to destabilize and reinvigorate technologies as they begin to lose their potential for change. Techniques move situations away from stability and serve as a catalyst for innovation.

Technological practice is a model for design that is capable of transforming and participating in technological change and is available for architects who are committed to architectural innovation. This model is predicated on the notion that techniques for design, as well as techniques for practice, are vital in order for innovation to be possible. Technological practices are comprised of six factors. First, they cross different technical and cultural lineages, affiliating architecture with the technological by using and inventing design techniques. These techniques are the foundation for a model of practice that is itself technological and positioned as an active and transformative entity operating within culture. In effect a catalyst for change, developing an interrelational, multi-lineage organization. Second, technological practice operates within the cultural milieu of its time, currently digital, and engages in the production and manufacturing of work as a cultural content. Third, design work develops from within technological and cultural change. Here technology is not applied onto to existing models of practice, instead, change is sought not only in the relationship between the work and the milieu in which it is situated, but in the very techniques and methods engaged in order to produce it. The traditional process of hypothesis, analysis, and intervention gives way to perpetual feedback between analysis, intervention and exchange with the environment. Because innovative design is technique-based, technological practices are capable of responding to cultural change and pressures over time, and are thus capable of acting as catalysts for culture in return. Technological practices seek to develop a more dynamic exchange and interactivity between the work and users.

The fourth factor for technological practice is that concepts are not developed prior to the act of designing, but arise from the continual feedback produced by the process itself. Fifth, technological practices operate across different scales and contexts. They encompass every scale from the molecular and material-based to the scale of the body, from individual building scale to the scale of the city. Their techniques are not dedicated to one scale or another, but are operative across numerous scales encompassing different technical lineages. Sixth, they re-contextualize techniques in a different lineage, to those already in existence with the lineage of architecture, to produce new effects for architecture in our current milieu. For example, boat builders have employed a technique of using geometry to describe and build the curvilinear contours of a boat hull for several centuries but have only recently been used to produce architecture. As far as architecture is concerned, these techniques have lain dormant for four hundred years. However, they are now a valuable dimension of innovation in the description and construction of contemporary architecture. Lastly, the effects that are produced by these inventive techniques affect culture in non-causal ways. These objectives are pursued through techniques and intelligence that generate positive feedback, learning and adapting across multiple disciplines and fields of knowledge.

Charles and Ray Eames established a technological practice in the mid-20th century. They crossed several disciplines and incorporated advances from material science, the automotive industry, aeronautics, hydraulics, film, the nascent computer industry and arts and media. External pressure from the Second World War enabled technical advancements that they appropriated to practice and develop the most sophisticated techniques of their time, and learned by inventing, designing and manufacturing. They were also fascinated with mass production, which was the most advanced method of manufacturing in their time. They applied their knowledge across varied scales from the production of splints, furniture, and exhibition designs to buildings.

The Eameses crossed several technical thresholds and lineages in the design and manufacturing of their furniture. Material science included the development of rubber, hydraulics and heating coils, glues, molded plywood and fiberglass, and techniques re-contextualized from the aeronautics and automotive industry. Henry Belter developed techniques for bending plywood in three directions in the 1850s, but it was not until the 1920s and 1930s that designers used it because of its usefulness as a relatively inexpensive material. Gerrit Rietveld, Alvar Aalto and Marcel Breuer all used bent plywood to make furniture, but it was always curved in one direction as the process for stable multidirectional bent plywood production was too technically difficult and the techniques required were not available.[8]

Shortly after 1941, Charles and Ray Eames developed an appropriate set of techniques and mechanisms for the inexpensive, but precise plywood molding with techniques borrowed from different disciplines. The "Kazam," a homemade machine that incorporated a rubber membrane inflated with a bicycle pump, pushed individual layers of wood against an electrically heated plaster mold. Multiple layers of wood were laminated together with the wood and glues coming from the MGM Studios lot where Charles Eames was employed in the set department. The Kazam enabled the Eameses to produce an unflawed chair from using a single piece of plywood molded into a compound form. Here the technical transforms to becoming technological, as it is immersed within a cultural context, and produces its own effects which contributes towards cultural efficacy.

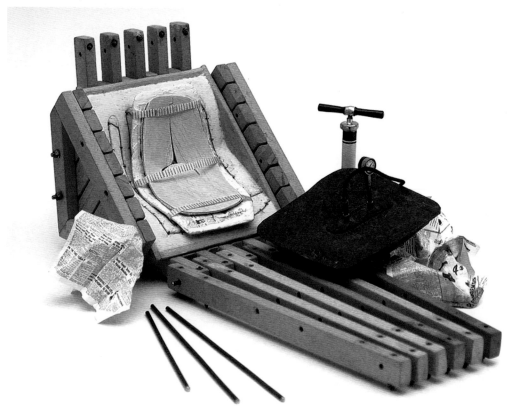

CHARLES EAMES AND RAY EAMES - "KAZAM! MACHINE"(1942)
© 2010 EAMES OFFICE LLC, FROM THE COLLECTIONS OF THE LIBRARY OF CONGRESS

The Eames' design and manufacturing of a leg splint also clearly demonstrates the crossing of technical lineages. During World War II, a scarcity of metal and the difficulty of maintaining sterile environments were resulting in a high number of amputations due to war injuries. This need rapidly accelerated the development of the Eames' plywood techniques. With assistance from the Navy the Eameses found that plywood was lightweight, easy to transport, and once molded would cushion injured legs properly, decreasing the rate of infection caused by metal splints that were difficult to sterilize from use to use. The Eameses produced a single prototype of a leg brace, molded from Charles's leg, and approached the Navy with a proposal to produce the splints for the war effort and were awarded a contract to produce 150,000 units. The Navy contract gave the Eameses access to classified information on synthetic adhesives and Allied plywood technology that had been developed for aviation purposes,[9] dramatically improving the quality of the molded pieces and making mass production possible. They were manufactured in 1942 and are credited with saving thousands of soldiers from amputation.

The technical know how that they gained while developing this splint was used in other contexts. High-frequency electronic welding developed at Chrysler to secure rubber shock mounts to plywood surfaces in order to join metal legs to the plywood seats and backs without any visible screws or fasteners accelerated the development of their furniture. This crossed the lineages of the automobile industry with their practice. These same techniques were employed in the Eames' later furniture pieces, notably the Eames lounge chair developed in 1956 as well as their fiberglass chairs. Later, the chairs were produced with hydraulic dyes used in the boat-building industry, yet another technical lineage that helped to reduce the cost of the chairs. This satisfied the Eames' ambition of participating in the cultural milieu of their time: that of mass production.[10]

Mass production was developed due to Fordist mentalities that pervaded the automobile industry in Detroit. Charles Eames had studied these plants in addition to the prefabricated automobile plants designed by Albert Kahn. Mass production was technically advanced, and only after the Eames practice was awarded the contract to manufacture splints for the Navy, did they become aware of the precise techniques that they would need to mass produce their plywood chairs. They applied this knowledge in the production of a fiberglass version of their earlier chairs. At first, each chair was laid up by hand using a conventional technique that the Eameses were familiar with from the glass cloth and resin panels they had developed for their own house, after which they collaborated with the Zenith Plastics Company and Herman Miller furniture company to develop a series of pieces for the Museum of Modern Art's Low Cost Furniture Design exhibition in 1948. Their fascination with the contemporary cultural milieu extended to their architecture. Their Pacific Palisades house was influential in bringing techniques of mechanized industrial production and mass production to the design and manufacturing of housing. The Eames House (1947-49) used prefabrication panels that were mass-produced. This method of production was adopted by the private sector after the war. Their solution solved the projected post-war housing shortage,[11] by incorporating prefabricated, standardized parts and industrial materials including steel trusses, fiberglass panels, plywood, and a repetitive and standardized window sash. Designed using pre-fabricated products that were available through catalogs, the entire structure of the house was erected in a day and a half.[12]

Their exhibition designs in 1961 at the California Museum of Science and Industry and in 1964 for the World's Fair in New York, both sponsored by IBM, crossed four very separate lineages, film, media theory, interface design, and the computer. Their interests in mathematics is evident by their first exhibition title "Mathematica: A World of Numbers and Beyond," after which they focused on the potential unleashed by the digital computer in "Think." This was only made possible by Douglas Engelbardt's invention of components for the graphical user interface, which was instrumental in creating new symbolic languages that would serve to overcome previous limitations that had existed between conceptual intentions and expression. This research was supported by JCR Licklider who had a vision developing a symbiotic partnership which would unleash tremendous creative potential, made possible with ease and immediacy through the flexibility of a keyboard and a real-time graphics display. This led to the formulation of a new language that expresses ideas and concepts through direct communication instead of communicating content through representation. This discovery unleashed creative potential.[13] The Eames' previous interests in film combined with their new interest in mathematics to produce a series of films for the exhibition at the California Museum of Science.

These two lineages also crossed with an earlier form of interactivity pioneered by Wagner, and developed by Maholy-Nagy- that of the Theater of Totality (1924), a reinterpretation of Richard Wagner's concept of *gesamtkunswerk*, or the total work of art. Maholy-Nagy's approach to the synthesis of the arts further reduced the importance of the written word and the presence of the actor, placing them on an equal plateau with stage design, lighting, music, and visual compositions. Underlying this approach was an effort to synthesize the theater's essential components; space, composition, motion, sound, movement, and light into a fully integrated, abstract form of artistic expression. All of these lineages were crossed to move the production of new effects within culture by incorporating multiple projection screens arrayed at various heights and angles, in addition to a "People Wall" accommodating

400 seated people, lifting them into an elliptical theater for the multi-screen, multimedia program that showed the latest computer technology at work. Here there was a complete removal of the actor, and the documentary film itself became the environment.

A critical point here is that the Eames' practice continually changed and adapted within their ever-changing cultural milieu, while restlessly exploring new lineages that can be crossed, or made to adapt to newer technologies that become available. They restlessly work within the present condition and forge towards the future to innovate and influence change. For example, as their practice was engaged in developing techniques for the manufacturing and production of their furniture and architecture, a new technology had become available. Their practice became increasingly interested in the development of the potential of computation and its ability to interact with the user communicating scientific advancements in legible and interesting ways. They assimilated and adapted to this new potential that they foresaw as being important to a changing future of culture. The way they engaged this potential was to work within this technology in time, becoming one with its potential for interactivity. While the Eames' practice is exemplary for the individual innovations they made, it is even more so for the breadth of their activities and the flexibility and interrelational quality of their techniques.

These criteria of technological practice are evident in the work of the Danish architect and designer Verner Panton. Panton appropriated techniques from the fine arts and material sciences. He operated in the culture of his time, which was mass production and an art world focused on popular culture. Panton worked within the potential of technology available to him and was focused on developing and transforming the furniture industry with designs that continually challenged the limits of what was in existence. The form of his work was inflected with his curiosity to further a material logic that was not in existence, guided by his curiosity for change and innovation. His work, like the Eames', also operates across many scales, from furniture to small and large interior projects.

Panton had developed a stackable and cantilevered chair in plywood for the WK European Furniture Design Competition in 1956 and was familiar with the techniques and limitations of plywood in the design of furnishings. He searched for a different material with the ability to be structurally more capable and lightweight than plywood. His eponymous chair was continually developed through an iterative process that spanned over forty years, encompassing numerous different lineages of material science and brought together with formal innovations that preceded their own ability to be manufactured. Panton became interested in the potential of plastics and other synthetic materials that were being used primarily as industrial material at the time, and had only recently become available for non-industrial uses.

What the Eameses had done in the 1950s with fiberglass and wood, Panton did for plastics and other synthetics in the 1970s. Materials that were being developed and made available to the marketplace in the late 1960s to mid 1970s can be traced back to the first plastics developed in the late 19th and early 20th centuries, but it was not until the 1950s that plastics were used in earnest in the production of consumer goods. The development of plastics follows a typical trajectory of technical refinement where different applications become increasingly limited as the materials are refined. Only occasionally do overlaps and crossed lineages occur, but their potential for acceptance and wide distribution is great. Marlex®, the trade name for crystalline polypropylene and high-density polyethylene (HDPE) plastics, was discovered in 1951 at Phillips Petroleum by scientists working on chemical additives for gasoline. This accidental

invention of Marlex® had occurred at a time when manufacturers were actively seeking more pliable and less brittle plastics than those available at the time. This innovation established Phillips as a major plastics manufacturer overnight. Panton crossed this lineage by re-contextualizing it within the furniture design industry.

In 1960 Panton developed a prototype of a cantilevered chair in extruded polystyrene, which was refined and developed, through ten iterations between 1960 and 1963.[14] By 1966, Panton began collaborating with Herman Miller and Vitra, the European licensee of Herman Miller's products, to develop the chair in different materials.[15] A version of the fiberglass chair was manufactured using a mechanized cold-press fiberglass-reinforced polyester resin in 1967, but the molded chairs were extremely heavy and had to be sanded and finished by hand. Panton's interest was to exploit the potential of the new material by contemporary mass production methods. A much lighter polyurethane foam version was developed the following year, but it still required hand-finishing. The advantage of this new material however, was that despite the hand-finishing, the chairs could be produced rapidly at a rate of one chair every thirty minutes, including the lacquering process. It was essential for Panton to offer the chair in as many colors as possible, as this was his interest intersecting with the pop art movement that was current at that time. The chair was finally offered in seven different lacquer colors.

His design methods continued to work within technology and at each point in the development of the chair its form was adjusted. Material experimentation over the course of his chair's development was equally dependant upon the availability of specific material characteristics. In early versions, the seat and back of the chair are relatively pronounced with the more curvilinear areas located on the sides and base. The form of the chair developed not only according to Panton's design directives, but in correspondence and in negotiation with the available material properties of specific plastic products. The chair design progressed with the invention of new materials. For this reason, as Panton's knowledge of the material and access to recent developments in plastics research grew, the chair's design progressed and the interval between the introduction of potentially useful plastic products and subsequent versions of the chair shrank. This can be seen with the introduction of the injection-molded thermoplastic version in 1971, here the chair developed into the smooth curvilinear surface that is familiar today. Structural ribs were added inside the base to ensure stability, then polyurethane foam became available in 1983. This newer lighter version developed into the next iteration in 1990 that was the mass-produced injection molded version of the chair in a matte finish that resisted scratching[16] became available. Panton's own interest in changing and adapting to the cultural milieu is clear.

Plastics and foam offered Panton the ability to experiment with a wide range of formal innovations, which he inflected with different body positions and configurations. Panton had consistently experimented with different spatial arrangements and their capacity to engender new social situations by manipulating the body's relationship to the furniture and interior environments. In effect, the user interacts with the environment that they are situated in. Integrated furniture pieces like the Living Tower or Pantower contained different seating areas at various heights and in different positions, encouraging users to engage it differently. He provided for the ability of different arrangements and different body positions to allow the user a new understanding of the space that was being inhabited.[17]

Panton's interior projects cross the different lineages contained within his practice from art, furniture design textile design and architecture. He incorporates explorations of form, color, lighting, and materials like plastics, fiberglass, clear plastics, steel, foam rubber and other synthetics, taking advantage of the new technologies of the post-war era. The experimental interior landscapes and environments he developed such as his Fantasy Landscape Room (so titled to express his desire to encourage users' fantasies for how their spaces might be used differently) sought to synthesize his interest in overcoming the traditional divisions of a room, dividing it into walls, floors, and ceilings. Panton's focus became an effort to undermine these divisions through a single unified design that had the capacity to be open to different uses and situations.

Both the Eamses and Panton identify techniques for technologies and contexts that are innovative for their time. Today, we find that the essential attributes of technological practices remain fundamentally unchanged. Historical examples are exemplary for their technique and their methods, but their context is different from ours. Designers today have many different techniques and technologies available to them as well as the potential of new developments in areas yet unknown. Naturally, contemporary techniques must be oriented toward innovation and the cross affiliation of technological advances and contexts by crossing the technical threshold.

Technological practices adopt the flexibility and nimble response to change, which is a feature of technology itself. Our current technology – digital technology makes the power of the computer available and offers the ability to produce a dynamic testing ground for complex and diverse constituencies. This is accomplished through the development of new techniques for using software not only for the purposes of generating form, but also to test different formal scenarios in different environments and to augment formal responses with the potential to influence

FACADE MODEL: GARMENT TOWER - GE YANG, YUNLONG ZHANG, HAO FU

culture through feedback. We all cross technical lineages in the production of new technologies. Re-appropriating software packages designed for other fields such as automotive, aeronautics and gaming industries is a crossing of many technical lineages itself. These software packages make new techniques of simulation in addition to a plethora of other techniques available to the architect. These techniques mingle with philosophy, science and mathematics, as well as automotive design, industrial design and digital animation industries. In particular, parametric-based modeling that is now available as a component of off-the-shelf modeling and animation software is well suited for the adaptability and flexibility that is a hallmark of technique-based technological practices. We find that these software packages are sophisticated enough to accommodate techniques that seek to simulate and then directly engage particular behaviors and occurrences, rather than seeking to represent them formally or pictorially. With the use and re-use of the software package developing digital techniques unleashes a series of new potentials that were not imagined prior to re-appropriating software packages. Innovation is furthered by each practice differently through experimentation of techniques instead of tradition. The practices themselves are adaptive; seeking to improve what has already been realized. Moving toward a model for design based on a technological practice takes full advantage of techniques and their ability to influence cultural efficacy. This not only reveals greater interrelational potential between technological, material, and cultural lineages, but profoundly increases their capacity to generate effects within culture.

Digital techniques generate technological development by putting pressures on and establishing new goals for technical refinement that, once situated within a context, become technological. The development of computer software is one example. Software is a technology, encompassing many lineages of computer programming and incorporating different subprograms, making them available to users. The programming of a computer in order to make it function is a largely technical activity composed of inputting commands. Software provides techniques in the form of tools and processes within the software itself, but in different contexts are applied towards different objectives. They are re-contextualized by different innovators with varied results. For example, if the same software package is used by different professionals. A musician might innovate using the software to generate music, while an architect may use it to develop intelligence in the production of form. New techniques are developed through the re-appropriation of software that is not originally intended for that use. These techniques transform the use of the technologies of software and computer, producing new unforeseen effects. The users have the possibility of identifying new technical thresholds that must be crossed in the future, informing the selection and development of new technologies.

Technological practices move away from representation, where one thing stands for something else to the degree that it is taken to be, for certain purposes, that second thing[18] and towards processes that employ the digital to simulate simple systems that produce synthetic and emergent wholes, organized from the bottom up, in addition to more top-down analytical approaches. Material production plays an important role as well. The current technology of manufacturing and construction is increasingly informed by design techniques and vice versa. A model for practice that understands architecture as technology, and the practice of architecture as a technological practice, aims to produce a continual negotiation between users and form, design content and manufacturing, and between architecture and its context, permitting greater occupational flexibility and allowing for the effects that result from techniques.

Techniques of manufacturing and construction that are more synthetic with the act of designing and the digital design environment are increasingly available. The increasing popularity of certain computer-aided-manufacturing processes is one indication of this potential. Technical applications such as numerically controlled milling and laser-cutting are influential not only as methods of production, but inform the development of techniques for design. Contemporary digital techniques of design and manufacturing have advanced to a point where design content is no longer subject to a fabrication process, or where techniques for fabrication are simply applied to a design.

The scope and significance of such change is potentially enormous. Technological choices give us a way to bridge the gap between the technical and the cultural, immersing one within the other. The feedback that is developed through this immersion creates a platform for innovation; the techniques that people generate through their use of technology exert pressure on technical refinement and enfold those refinements within culture.

[1] Larry A. Hickman, *Philosophical Tools for Technological Culture, Putting Pragmatism to Work* (Bloomington: Indiana University Press, 2001).

[2] Stephen Jay Gould, *Bully for Brontosaurus* (New York: Norton, 1991) 65.

[3] Gilles Deleuze, *Francis Bacon: The Logic of Sensation* (Minneapolis: University of Minnesota Press, 2002) 139.

[4] Geoffrey D. Austrian, *Herman Hollerith: Forgotten Giant of Information Processing* (New York: Columbia University Press, 1982).

[5] Paul Ceruzzi, *A History of Modern Computing* (Cambidge: MIT Press, 2003) 122.

[6] Gilles Deleuze, ibid, 138.

[7] Gilles Deleuze, ibid, 138.

[8] Pat Kirkham, *Charles and Ray Eames: Designers of the Twentieth Century* (Cambridge: MIT Press, 1996) 207.

[9] Pat Kirkham, ibid, 209.

[10] Pat Kirkham, ibid, 236.

[11] John Neuhart, Marilyn Neuhart, Ray Eames, *Eames Design: The Work of the Offices of Charles and Ray Eames*, (London: Thames and Hudson, 1998) 22.

[12] James Steele, *Eames House: Charles and Ray Eames*, (London: Phaidon Press, 2002) 10.

[13] Douglas Engelbardt, Lecture at the San Francisco Musuem of Modern Art, 1996.

[14] "Verner Panton Resource Pack," (London: Design Musuem, 2001) 2

[15] "Verner Panton Resource Pack," (London: Design Musuem, 2001) 4

[16] "Verner Panton" from A Century of Chairs, (London: Design Museum, 2003), http://www.designmuseum.org.uk/designerex/verner-panton.htm

[17] Alexander von Vegesack and Mathias Remmele, *Verner Panton: The Collected Works*, (Weil am Rhein: Vitra Design Museum, 2000).

[18] Elizabeth Mertz and Richard Parmentier, *Semiotic Mediation: Sociocultural and Psychological Perspectives*, (Orlando: Orlando Academic Press, 1985) 209.

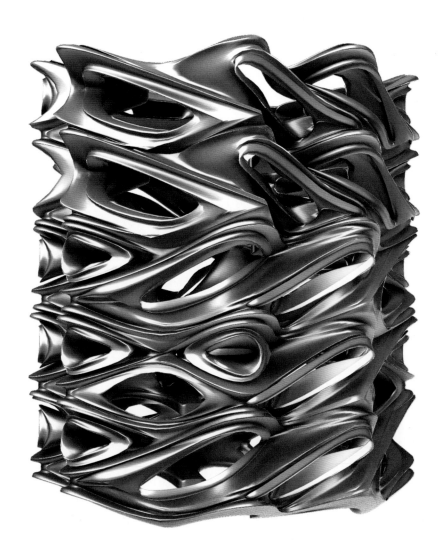

FACADE MODEL: SPEED TRADER - ANDRES DANIEL CELY, TIANYI SUN, YUHAN BIAN

MATTHEW SOULES

FORM AGAINST FINANCE?

Financialization changes architectural space in a myriad of ways to make it perform better as an investment asset and synthetically co-exist with shifts in a complex milieu of laws, regulations, and behaviors. Perhaps the single biggest component of this transformation is the drive to make architectural spaces fungible and liquid asset – that is, to make it increasingly standardized and simplified so that it can be easily bought, sold, and owned like other asset categories, such as stocks. What is the role of architectural form in this process? More specifically, what is its role in the pursuit of fungibility and liquidity? Three common tactics in the drive toward fungibility and liquidity can be identified: diminished sociality, simplified ownership, and abstracted locality. Each of these tactics has a formal dimension and the projects collected in this book provide a timely opportunity to consider potential answers to this question.

Compared to other asset types, architectural space is remarkably heterogeneous – it is at the opposite end of the spectrum from say, a barrel of oil, which is always the same from barrel-to-barrel. Much of architecture's diversity is unavoidable, like the difference that geographic location lends, from city-to-city for example. But some can be diminished – like the unpredictability and diversity that human inhabitants themselves bring to architectural space. It is possible, of course, through planning and space making decisions, to reduce the ability for inhabitants to interact in a building and this enervation has the effect of standardizing the increments of architectural investment. Form can thus diminish the possibility of sociality and thereby further financialization.

Many of the most optimum financial assets are relatively easy to own. An individual stock equity, for example, is an immaterial, low-cost way in which an individual can own a portion of a much larger and complicated corporate entity. In contrast, the physical character of real estate typically involves a host of directly time-consuming engagements with it – such as those associated with its physical security, maintenance, and upkeep. As architecture is financialized there is an impetus to employ characteristics that diminish the necessity of these physical engagements.

At the same time that architecture is standardized, homogenized, physically disengaged and unencumbered, it is paradoxically made to appear more unique and locally specific. This fabrication of locality compensates for the degree to which the tendencies to enhance the asset function of architecture can themselves render an asset undesirable. New localitiesare the means by which real estate keeps its stake in the "real" by not entirely becoming another asset category. The invented forms of reality are by design more singular and simpler than preceding versions, this abstraction facilitates a higher degree of control, predictability, and stability.

If diminished sociality, simplified ownership, and abstracted locality are all ways that form is employed to further financialization, it is compelling to consider how form might challenge or counter these architectural logics of financialization? While the work collected in this publication is not overtly aimed at countering financialization, it nevertheless provides an opportunity to explore this issue. And because the way that the contemporary tall slender tower tends to diminish sociality, simplify ownership, and generate abstract localities, it is itself a preferred form of financialization. The work included here addresses the question of formal financialization by looking at the center of the storm—the pencil tower. The work's consistently intenseinterest in the role form itself can be related to the notion of "asset" by necessity foregrounds the question of what form can do in relation to the function of an asset. The following emerges from the work.

Collective Entanglements

The tall and slender condo tower is a form that inherently reduces social interaction in the building interior through proportions that reduce the floor area and, by extension, the number of discrete units on any given floor. Few units per floor has the effect of diminishing the likelihood of direct interaction with others but also the perceptual presence of others through indirect stimuluslike sounds, smells, and vibrations. Given the tendency for finance to move architectural space towards something akin to a post-social condition, one possible point of confrontation is for architecture to assert new possibilities of collective entanglement through the use of form. Many of the projects included in this book seem to do just that. The interior of "Invisible Tower," for instance, proposes a central interior void in which circulation from discrete units is sensorially unified. "Vertical Mausoleum" offers another form of entanglement – instead of a single interconnected space, the section reveals a series of interlocking and nested interior volumes that makes possible sensing the presenceof other users. Many of the other projectsare ambitious in shaping space for shared collective interiority. Who knows what kind of collective life could unfold in these spaces – but clearly it is the antithesis to the standardized and discretely layered interiors of financialized form. Perhaps collective entanglements might arise that could themselves be a challenge to fungibility and by extension, financialization?

Private Repairs

One of the reasons that condominiums are especially attractive to investors is that they collectivize maintenance activities through the management of the strata board. Individual unit owners are relatively liberated from building upkeep concerns. But this is not only a housing tenure and management consideration – it all also relates to scale, organization, and form. In comparison to the detached home with its yard and entirely exposed envelope that operates at the scale of the individual housing unit, the multi-unit structure reduces the landscape to interior ratio while diminishing the amount of exterior envelope

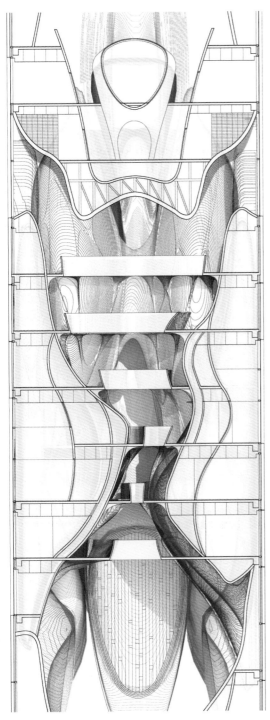

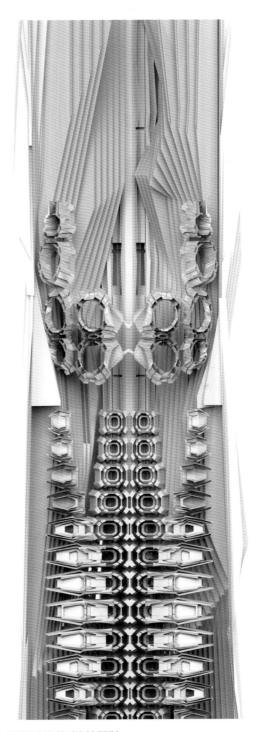

INVISIBLE TOWER
ALI TABATABAIE GHOMI, YUCHI WANG, MEARI KIM

VERTICAL MAUSOLEUM
BOSUNG JEON, CARRIE ROSE FRATTALI, XIAOYU ZHAO

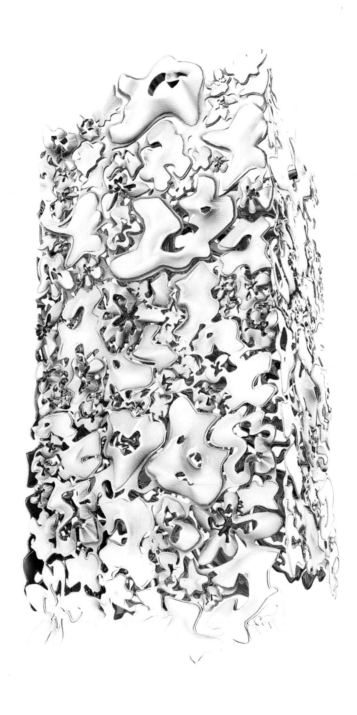

FACADE DETAIL: NESTED MORPH - SIYANG LV, CAN WANG, YUCHEN ZHAO, SOOKWAN AHN

connected to any one unit. This is most evident with the roof – a major point of failure and concern in the single family home. A tower, in contrasts, can pack hundred of units under one small roof area which diminishesthe per unit responsibility for failure to a comparably minimal level. The direct performancebenefits of this notwithstanding, it has the byproduct of making the condo tower unit easier to own remotely and thereby more effectively act as an investment asset.

An opportunity to challenge this type of disengagement with the individual unit could be to intentionally generate opportunities of maintenance and repair that are non-collectivized and directly connected spatially with the unit. Of course, to do so is anathema to the contemporary ethos of multi-unit housing but what if the benefits were significant? What is needed is akin to the detached-home's one-to-one relationship with its roof and garden metamorphasized into a tower condition of serial organization. However, this does not literally translate into a tower in which each unit gets its own roof or garden – as one finds in James Wines' High-rise of Homes. A conceptual and formal mutation is required. But might theremarkable surface geometries many of the projects in this book represent that mutation? What if the surface of let's say, "Nested Morph," was correlated to interior unit distribution in such a way that afforded individuated unit-based opportunities for new types of engagement with the skin and its exterior, and by extension, maintenance of the skin and its folds and undulations? Individuated ownership extended into surface topology—almost like a new form of merged garden and roof.

An opportunity to challenge this type of disengagement with the individual unit could be to intentionally generate opportunities of maintenance and repair that are non-collectivized and directly connected spatially with the unit. Of course, to do so is anathema to the contemporary ethos of multi-unit housing but what if

the benefits were significant? What is needed is akin to the detached-home's one-to-one relationship with its roof and garden metamorphasized into a tower condition of serial organization. However, this does not literally translate into a tower in which each unit gets its own roof or garden — as one finds in James Wines' *High-rise* of Homes. A conceptual and formal mutation is required. But might theremarkable surface geometries many of the projects in this book represent that mutation? What if the surface of let's say, "Nested Morph", was correlated to interior unit distribution in such a way that afforded individuated unit-based opportunities for new types of engagement with the skin and its exterior, and by extension, maintenance of the skin and its folds and undulations? Individuated ownership extended into surface topology—almost like a new form of merged garden and roof.

Intense Locality

Financialized space tends to compensate for its standardization and post-social character by deploying abstract localities that provide a semblance of authenticity. This condition is sometimes achieved withformal and material strategies that obscure homogeneity. For example, the Jane Jacobs influenced character of many sidewalk-fronting podiums that mask the generic standardization of the condo towers rising above. Or nostalgic skins replete with diverse materiality that conceal spatial homogeneity. But perhaps the most preferred form of generating locality is through the obsessive provision of views. A view is always somehow unique and by necessity offers a degree of local specificity. But when considered in a spectrum of other possible local attributes, the view is a relatively distant and removed attribute that is only always optical – for these reasons it is comparably abstract. This type of abstract locality offers relative predictability and therefore stability in comparison with other types of local specificity. In contrast to abstract localities, perhaps the generation of new intense localities that provide a more meaningful differentiation could counter the logics and practice of financialization? Could the morphological diversity within "The Abyss" or "Hephaestus" constitute the creation of local variation that is significant enough to problematize finance in some way? This relies on the locality being different enough – but no so different to undermine the economies of scale that make multi-unit housing attractive in the first place. "Speedtrader" offers an interesting example in this regard. In this project, the thickened skin's particular directionality promises to lend distinct visual, environmental, and spatial attributes to each unit, thereby radically departing from the standardized attributes that define condo units as investment assets. This type of proliferating formal localities in the building itself make it harder for the units to be treated as tradable commodities.

The Necessity of Non-Normative Form

It would seem that architectural form could possess the capability to confront the seemingly inexorable forces of financialization by essentially slowing down the move towards increasingly fungible and liquid space. By subtly shapingarchitectural conditions such that they require individuated upkeep and therefore contact, enable heightened social interaction, and are significantly unique, the easily owned and traded commodity character of asset oriented architecture is challenged. But to what degree can these factors alone truly challenge finance? Clearly they are just one aspect of anincredibly complex phenomenon and therefore any potential mitigation must be relatively minor. Interestingly, the capacity of form to challenge finance as conceptualized here is by way of it impacting behavior around it – be it maintenance orsocial interaction. But what about form unto itself – in a deeply autonomous sense?

One of the enviable and yet maddening traits of capitalism is its capacity to voraciously incorporate endlessly diverse and even anti-capitalist conditions into its mode of operations. What is a radical affront to capitalism one day is a whole new lifestyle consumer category the next day. Even if the forms described here were ultra-effective at challenging finance today, there is good reason to believe they would be far less so in the years to come. This raises the obvious question of what good is formal innovation at all if it is just a matter of time before it is co-opted?

Perhaps the answer resides in the notion of radical innovation itself? That is, substantial non-normativity can itself be an affront to the forces of capitalism. The novelty of certain formal conditions precludes fungibility because of their sheer foreignness. Of course, novelty and innovation are requisites of capital growth trajectories making this a perilous counter position to occupy, always fraught with the possibility of it becoming its other. Any formal novelty therefore must exist in a way that challenges the needs of capital at the moment of its deployment—with the full knowledge that those needs will evolve in the future to render the formal position ineffectual as a functional critique of capital. The work of *Asset Architecture 3* can be understood to pursue a set of formal investigations that challenge the functional requirements of capital now. Maybe one of the most exciting aspects of the work is not only how it exists in the present, but what it projects as its next avatar tomorrow?

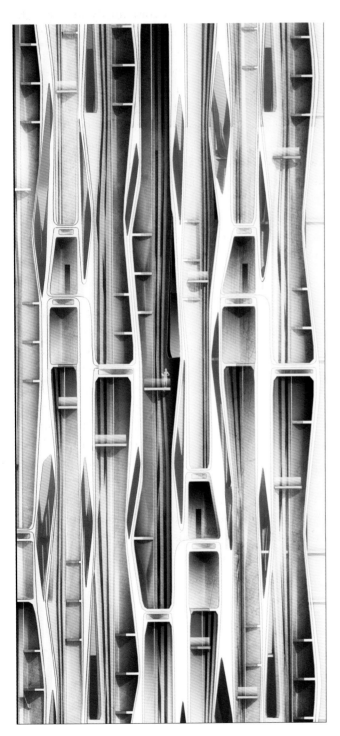

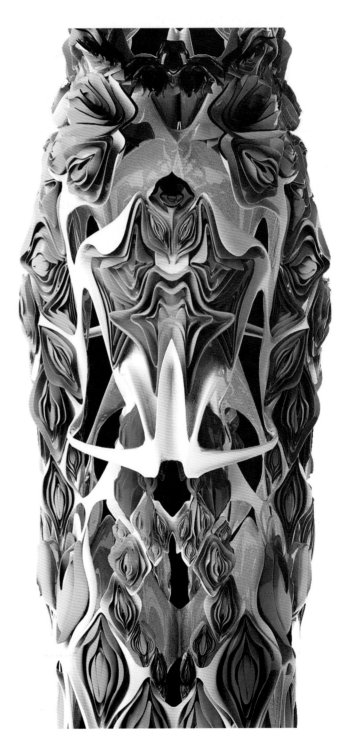

THE ABYSS - ANGELIKI TZIFA, KE LIU, DONGLIANG LI   HEPHAESTUS - SHUOQI XIONG, KAI TANG, JIA LYU

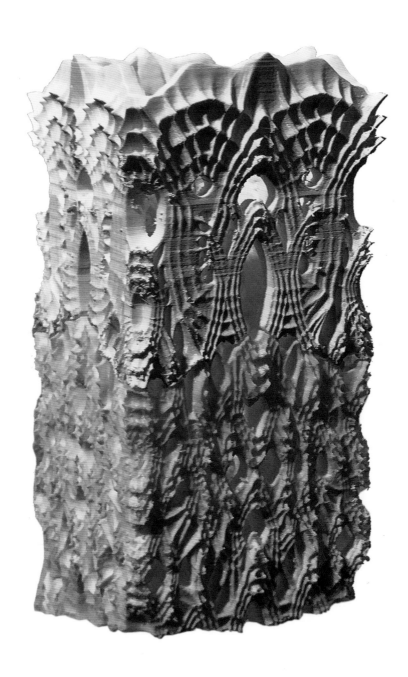

FACADE DETAIL: ONE VENTURE CAPITAL - TAESEO PARK, MUSAB MOHAMMAD, XIAOYI GAO

ROBERT NEUMAYR

THE BEST BUILDING MONEY CAN BUY

"Once you learn to look at architecture not merely as an art more or less well or more or less badly done, but as a social manifestation, the critical eye becomes clairvoyant."

— Louis Sullivan

In 1896 Dankmar Adler and Louis Sullivan completed what would eventually be their practice's last major built project, the Guaranty Building in downtown Buffalo. At the time of its completion however, the building had already changed its name. Carefully located at the intersection of Church and Pearl Street close to most of the city's and the county's official buildings, it was initially supposed to be called the Taylor Building, named after a local businessman by the name of Hascal T. Taylor, who had developed the early skyscraper as a speculative office building in the wake of the construction boom surrounding Buffalo's quick but temporary rise to importance as its former mayor Grover Cleveland was elected 22nd president of the United States.

It was only due to the entrepreneur's untimely death before the structure's completion that the contracted Guaranty Construction Company decided to continue with the project alone. But also, the architectural firm Adler & Sullivan met its fate. Ironically enough, a continuous decline in commissions, resulting from a severe recession, known as the Panic of 1893, that in turn started with the burst of a speculative bubble in Argentina, forced the two architects to dissolve their partnership in 1894.

So, speculation, I would argue, has from early on been one of the key drivers for real estate development in general but also for its most prominent protagonist in particular: the urban skyscraper. However, little attention has been given to the question of how the principles of financial speculation have affected its historic and typological development.

In her book *Form Follows Finance*, Carol Willis for example argues that high-rise buildings, especially in Chicago and New York, have always been speculative developments, and that their form, location, and distribution throughout the city are the result of the complex interactions of parameters such as plot sizes, local or regional building patterns, cost effective construction technologies, fluctuating real estate cycles, building codes and zoning laws.[1]

Christopher Marcinkoski defines speculative urbanization as "[...] the construction of urban infrastructure or settlement for political or economic purposes, rather than to meet real (as opposed to artificially exaggerated) demographic or market demand".[2] Providing an overview of notable past and present speculation bubbles, he points out a fundamental change in what drives contemporary urban development. Urbanization is no longer a response to economic growth but is rather deployed as a driver for economic growth, thus becoming a preferred instrument of economic production.

As the amount of capital that is channeled towards real estate increases, the degree to which space functions as an asset has increased radically and the large-scale effects, that high-rise buildings as objects of financial investments have on their immediate built environment become visibly more clearly. It seems that cities nowadays have become complexly multi-layered commercial environments, where space is being privatized in all three dimensions and all property – similar to the stock market – is subject to fluctuating value cycles. Buildings have become assets and air rights have developed into a speculative commodity.

In that sense, for some time now, New York, and more specifically Manhattan, with its long history of converting incoming capital to high density building mass, has been on the forefront of this development and therefore seems to be uniquely equipped as a location to examine the phenomena of speculation, asset architecture and its effects.

In direct contradiction to the standard evaluation criteria typically associated with any building in an urban context, the contemporary pencil shaped condominium towers that sprout all over the city, only operate as financial investment assets. Following the national trend, speculative vacancy in New York has grown rapidly to 12% of the housing market[3] and explains why so many

facade windows of upscale Fifth, Madison, and Park Avenue apartment buildings remain dark every evening. In 2004 across the United States 23 percent of all the houses acquired were for investment purposes and another 13 percent were obtained as second homes.[4]

As of now, New York is still the third most expensive city for prime real estate in the world. According to Knight Frank Research,[5] in December 2016 one million USD allows you to buy 26m² of prime property. At that time only Monaco and Hong Kong did better. For the amount of one million USD you could afford 20m² of luxurious property, in the exclusive Mediterranean princedom that same amount of money bought you a meagre 17m² of first class real estate. But cities in the Western hemisphere appear to be on the decline, and Asia seems to be on the rise. In 2016 luxury residential market performance in New York was at a 3.50 percent and market value is forecast to not increase at all in 2017. In comparison, the four top performing cities in the Prime International Residential Index (PIRI) 2016 were all Asian, Shanghai coming in first, closely followed by Beijing and Guangzhou (all three of them with an increase of prime real estate value of around 27 percent) and Seoul. And contrary to New York, Shanghai's top real estate segment is predicted to increase in value by another eight percent in 2017.[6]

It was only recently, and after looking back at a considerable record of burst real estate bubbles, that the notion of financial speculation as the main driver for urban tower development has started to rapidly gain influence within the contemporary discourse about high-rise structures within an urban context, considerably shifting the way we look at the history of the skyscraper. More than any other contemporary building typology, the tower has always been widely understood, by the general public as well as within the profession, as a symbol for innovation, modernity, technological advancements, and progress. As a consequence, historically, two narratives dominated the discourse about the development of the skyscraper. The first account is chronological, understanding the tower as in itself a shapeless typology that adapts throughout history to the prevailing styles, ideas and agendas of any given specific time period. The second reading focuses on technological aspects, linking constant advances in building and construction technology as the main drivers behind skyscraper development. However as both of these narratives can only operate post festum, they lack the projective mechanisms that would be needed to allow for productive speculations about this dynamic typology's future.

But now, as these narratives are being cast aside by an increasing criticism of global capitalism, its relation to speculative capital, global wealth distribution and its impact on our built environment, high-rise buildings are rediscovered as ideological objects to bring back a strong social and political agenda to architecture, tying in with modernism's long lost social project, where rationalization, new technologies, automated production techniques and innovative materials were supposed to provide affordable high-quality products and solve social problems on a global scale.

So, while the contemporary architectural production, such as Norman Foster's 700-foot ultra-thin high-tech residential tower on 610 Lexington Avenue, just behind Mies van der Rohe's Seagram Building, is still well embedded within the current architectural paradigm and its speculative logic, shifting the architectural discourse back towards a more socially biased agenda has also jump-started academic speculation about the socially responsible future of the skyscraper, following Zaha's famous dictum that "[w]ithout experimentation not much can be discovered. [...] I think there should be no end to experimentation".[7] And in its more interesting recent moments, the results of these experimental design approaches manage to be innovative on multiple levels.

"New York Horizon", the winning entry of the 2016 Evolo Scyscraper Competition,[8] for example, explores a new high-rise typology by excavating Central Park down to its bedrock, thus creating a seven-mile-long and 1000 feet tall wall of skyscrapers along its perimeter, with an unobstructed view onto the newly emerging underground landscape.

Referring to one of Central Park's designers, Frederick L. Olmsted's initial intention, to provide a central common green space, equally accessible to all citizens, the project clearly sets its social agenda in providing an additional seven square miles of inhabitable indoor space with direct view to the park scenery, a commodity that has become scarce in recent years as new towers around Central Park have continued to rise higher than ever before as have the prizes of property with a direct view to it.

By doing so, at the same time, the project inverts the modernist understanding of the relationship between building and landscape, making the purposefully faceless architecture the mere background for the natural landscape as a centerpiece. But, just like the "Manhattan Tower," a twelve-kilometer-high extrusion of the "site formerly known as Central Park, scraping the Stratosphere" in Jimenez Lai's dystopian graphic novel *Babel*,[9] the proposal also makes us reconsider our understanding of scale and the reciprocity between volume and void. It reveals the complex interplay between the height limits of large-scale human structures and the immediate, yet not directly graspable dimensions of the geological and geographical structures that surround us and it reminds us of the unearthed potentials of the contemporary urban fabric's inherently stratified nature and vertical complexity.

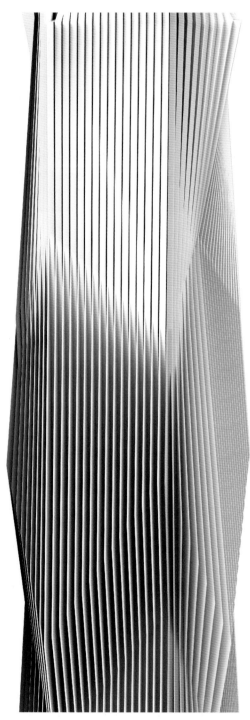

VERTICAL MAUSOLEUM
BOSUNG JEON, CARRIE ROSE FRATTALI, XIAOYU ZHAO

ONE MILLION TOWER
JIANGBAO ZHONG, MENGYUE WU, XIAONAN CHEN

This year's MSD-AAD students responded to the design brief in equally innovative ways, speculating about how novel ideas about asset driven architecture could start to shape the program, structure, materiality, form, and visual nature of the contemporary city tower.

Responding to the prevailing speculative urban high-rise development, the studio's thesis is how to design a Manhattan skyscraper that, rather than fighting financial investment logic, subversively operates within the capitalist paradigm in order to come up with building proposals that will not only generate a return on investment that outperforms conventional investment strategies, but that will also at the same time be able to operate as a social, cultural, or programmatic condenser within the surrounding city fabric.

Understanding the mechanics of asset architecture as a complex social phenomenon rather than an abstract and detached market mechanism, students are able to conceptualize the given challenge simultaneously on a social, cultural, programmatic and aesthetic level.

A series of seven sites in midtown Manhattan along the south end of Central Park that form part of Billionaires Row, becomes the testing ground for this semester's speculative design research.

Some teams investigate alternative programs that might lend themselves as possible investments and their potential to be organized in new vertical ways.

Starting from the observation that burial space has become a scarce commodity in New York, leaving only one cemetery still selling space for remains on the crowded island of Manhattan, the project "Vertical Mausoleum" by students Carrie Frattali, Jeon Bosung, and Zhao Xiaoyu for example investigates a novel type of real estate by turning burial space into a commodity and developing it as a vertical program.

The vertically structured mausoleum can produce a huge variety of burial typologies at varying price levels, depending on prominence, orientation, views or relativity to ceremonial or public spaces. Vertical, densely stacked mausoleums, niches, stacks of urns or caskets are contained within the structural elements of the building and connected by a procession of programs. The tower's novel typology rotates the traditional ceremonial progression into verticality, thus elevating the process of ritual, meditation, and contemplation in a vertical version of the traditional landscaped cemeteries. The towers facade consists of a series of louvers that change direction and depth, highlighting program changes on the interior as well as providing a variety of light quality throughout the tower.

Another important field of research appears to be the investigation into new residential typologies. With new condominium towers going up across the city nowadays in the form of super slim pencil towers, the floor plans of New York's most expensive apartments have locked into one standardized one-story layouts that wrap around a massive central core, increasingly failing to offer differentiated experiences in a saturated market.

"The Abyss," a project by students Li Dongliang, Liu Ke, and Angelika Tzifa sets out to redefine the concept of luxury housing by developing an interiority of accentuated verticality, that reflects the soaring upright directionality of the tall building's overall shape. 136 apartments units are devised with minimized footprints on multiple levels, which are connected internally by a moving platform. They are stacked and arranged following a vertical packing algorithm to interlock around a series of vertical void spaces that act as atria for the respective units.

Other design projects finally call into question the well-established financing models for contemporary asset architecture. "Ten Million New York" by students Chen Xiaonan, Wu Mengyue, and Zhong Jianbao for example suggest a participatory bottom-up real estate crowd funding model in which a multitude of small private investors contribute a modest investment to the overall cost of the skyscraper. In return, they do not only receive tradeable shares of the building but also gain the exclusive right to access the tower and its semi-private facilities which are being shared by all the investors. The building's interiority in turn consists of a vastly different spaces, levels, plateaus, niches, and crevices generating a multiplicity of atmospheres with their respective effective and affective conditions to be temporarily inhabited by its shareholders.

Consequentially the continuously variegated outdoor space that entwines the building, reads as a complex contemporary three-dimensional interpretation of New York's private green spaces, such as Gramercy Park.

[1] Carol Willis, *Form Follows Finance. Skyscrapers and Skylines in New York and Chicago* (New York: Princeton Architectural Press, 1995).

[2] Christopher Marcinkoski, *The City That Never Was* (New York: Princeton Architectural Press, 2015).

[3] Sam Roberts, "Homes Dark and Lifeless, Kept by Out-of-Towners" *The New York Times*, 06 July 2011. Online edition.

[4] "In Come the Waves" *Economist*, 06 November 2008. http://www.economist.com/node/12501011.

[5] Kate Everett-Allen, "Going up, going down," *The Wealth Report 2017*. Ed. Andrew Shirley, (London: KnightFrank, 2017).

[6] James Roberts, "Future view," *The Wealth Report 2017*. Ed. Andrew Shirley. (London: KnightFrank, 2017).

[7] Hans Ulrich Obrist, "Foreword," *Zaha Hadid Early Paintings and Drawings*, (London: Serpentine Galleries and Koenig Books, 2016).

[8] "New York Horizons" *Evolo Skyscraper Competition 2016*. http://www.evolo.us/competition/new-york-horizon/.

[9] Jimenez Lai, "Babel," *Citizens of No Place. An Architectural Graphic Novel*. (New York: Princeton Architectural Press, 2012).

TOM VEREBES

THE PARADIGMS OF POLITICS AND PRIVATIZATION
– FROM RAYMOND HOOD TO ROBIN HOOD

"Now some of you might think that our loyal host intended this treasure for the coffers of Prince John, instead of to ransom the king—and you'd be right. But a strange thing happened. A change of heart overtook him in the forest and there it is safe and sound."
— *The Adventures of Robin Hood*
Written by Norman Reilly;
Directed by Michael Curtiz,
William Keighley, 1838

Architecture Versus the City: NY-LON-KONG

Asset architecture accelerates the commodification of architecture, in which the privacy, protection and proliferation of personal wealth is prioritized well ahead of the public civic and cultural dividends of vast private investment. Far from limited to the island of Manhattan, there has been an increasing global tendency for architecture to serve, and in turn, for architects themselves to serve, as facilitators of the valet parking of piles of cash in monolithic, fortress-like extruded disruptions into cities. In the case of New York, the air rights of these relatively small, single plots, found now to be distributed opportunistically within the Manhattan grid, present little evidence of planning on the city-scale.

Shopping malls, along with other types of internalized and commercialized urbanism, as so-called privately owned, managed and policed public space, is a discounted, or short-changed mutation of the seemingly old-fashioned notion of public urban space. At the risk of naïveté, this example of the commercialization of urbanism is at once a degradation of urban architecture as a mere tool for investment on discrete infill parcels of land. In Manhattan, land, in advance of its maximization as architecture, is a precious commodity, which has great power to proliferate wealth, limited to the fortunate few. Perhaps, at this juncture, it may be understood as alarmist and retrograde, even nostalgic, to cry for the voice of civics and community in the city. Do the consequences of asset architecture include the relinquishing of the planning and regulatory regimes of urban governance, which serve the largest demography for the greatest good? Righteous, resistant voices may yell, possibly in vain, in the heads of fuddy-duddy architects and urbanists, "Vive la résistance!"; and "Power to the People!". Is La Résistance to architecture as asset, on behalf of the have-nots, too late? In the face of the commodification of architecture, are the only options and the city, surrender, or worse, complicity?

Ny-lon-kong

In January 2008, still several months before the momentum gathered and the full force of what became known as the Global Financial Crisis had occurred, *Time Magazine* ran a feature article and dedicated its cover with a title reading, "Ny-lon-kong: How three connected cities drive the local economy. The keys to their success—and the challenges they now face."[1] Ny-lon-kong is an acronym for New York-London-Hong Kong. These cities, along with other post-industrial global urban centers, where the flow of vast quantities of capital is concentrated and generated, are also some of the world's most important nodes for culture and creativity. Ny-long-kong, both conceptually and practically, emphasizes the centrality of a few key locales, in the mobility and concentration of global capital, and also of the cultural development in a post-industrial context. Amidst the arbiters of neoliberal,

laissez faire economics resides the power of these cities to profoundly shape, transform and innovate upon the creative expression of the architecture of the city.

A Paradoxical Context

In this urban and architectural context, a series of paradoxes arise. As introduced earlier, the evidence of conflicts of interest exist between the private ownership of discrete architecture, and the collective, public ownership of the city as a continuous space. In asset architecture, the discreetness of the individual, inten-sive building block, rests obtusely within the extensive Manhattan grid and its buildings. Writing on the grid of Manhattan, Rem Koolhaas understand it as "a new balance between control and de-control in which the city can be at the same time ordered and fluid and a metropolis of rigid chaos."[2] If Asset Architecture is an extreme privatization of architectural space, to what extent might a public urbanism of the cultural life of the city coexist alongside and within these exclusive delineations?

In the journal, *Asset Architecture 1*, David Ruy's insightful commentary on the seeming dualities of culture and economy, champions architecture to persist as a preeminent creative endeavor with immense cultural merits, despite being intertwined with great complexity with its economic value.[3] Questions arise in this regard, as to the extent to which creative practices are service industries or cultural industries. Interestingly, architecture occu-pies a privileged remaining vestige of material valued as wealth, in sharp contrast to the immaterial processes of the economy, in how money today is dematerialized, existing only as 1s and 0s in a computa-tional matrix of exchange and tabulation.

A darker, and more disturbing absence of a duality, between utopia, and its opposite, which had persisted for centuries, cannot be ignored in this context. Christopher Hight's fictive narrative of a dystopia future for urbanity is at once a gripping and poetic literary urban tragedy.[4] Since asset architecture is situated in time and space in an ongoing condition of postmodernity, utopia, as an ideal state of urban society, fails to ex-plain the present nor future context of asset architecture, nor serve much pertinence. In fact, the anti-utopia idea of the city, as Colin Rowe and Fred Koetter explicated so eloquently in *Collage City*, as the grappling with the city as an existing, complex and problematic set of conditions, rather than an ideal state.[5] Asset architecture seeks to internalize a private and personal luxurious utopia, creating further complications for the staging of architecture as a public commodity in the city.

The politics, economics and social order of accelerationism was, at least in the old school of the 1990s, an era of optimism for the cultural and social progress, understood to be delivered through technological innovation and the new networked economy. During the three years of the AAD's asset architecture agenda, Donald Trump was elected president, and the UK voted to exit the European Union. Political leaders such as Vladimir Putin, Xi Jinping, Kim Jung-Un, Viktor Orban, along with a handful of other wannabes such as Nigel Farage and Marie Le Pen, represent the trajectory of a retreat from openness, tolerance and optimism, towards an increasingly hostile political sphere, in which neoliberal capitalism is understood as the motor of social acceleration. As Sanford Kwinter eloquently states, "it is no longer the thermonuclear bomb with its particular modes of geopolitical rationality, that is shaping our consciousness, but a new numeric parametric one: the Market."[6] In the face of the free market in the rise of an ecological consciousness which has complicated the polarity of political stances. Although a contemporary context can be characterized by the obsolescence of the simple spectrum of left and right, two models of twentieth century urbanism were promoted by the two great superpowers of the Cold War, Capitalist New York, and Soviet Moscow.[7] Clearly the capitalist model reigned supreme and supplanted the micro districts of Moscow and also the Danwei work units of Chinese cities. These moves away from collectivization, towards libertarianism, in the context of urbanism, begs for effective public governance, to grab back power from greed, to advocate for the public benefit of the dynamics of the free-market. With great irony, the Non-Planning Movement of the 1960s ushered in modernism's ultimate demise through an extreme of laissez-faire urbanism expressing personal freedom and a decidedly counteraction to the paternalism of the welfare state.[8] Charles Jencks' 1969 project, Consumer Democracy, sought for a connected personal and urban space through telecommunications, depicting a cartoon version of internet shopping decades later. Ultimately a form of consumerism which foresaw a supply-led rather than demand based economy, this trajectory is evident in the unregulated neoliberal investment frenzy into asset architecture unleashed in Ny-lon-kong. Patrick Schumacher, in his article, "Free Market Urbanism – Urbanism beyond Planning," asks rhetorically, "Is urbanism at all possible in the face of free market dynamism?."[9] Urbanism is more complicated, given the complicity of asset architecture.

Urban Design Thinking and the Art of the Deal

Design thinking in business, finance and real estate worlds emphasizes questioning norms and conventions and focusing on the end-users, in modes which encourage participatory models of decision making. Financial speculation has its parallels to the varied approaches to design innovation. In this light, the AAD's speculations are radical exchanges between wholly unfamiliar architectural models and their corresponding speculative financial models. Architecture here acts as the curator of a manifold of flows of information between technology and culture.

In Donald Trump and Tony Schwartz's book, *The Art of the Deal*, the celebration of loopholes and trade-offs are presented as a model for winning, rather than win-winning.[10] Whatever happened to the art of deal-making between investors in architecture and the political regulators of urbanism, with the interest of the public always in mind? In the making of the Rockefeller Center in the 1930s, by the architect Raymond Hood, deals were made between the planning bodies and the developers, which created what Sigfried Giedion called "an ideal community center."[11] The augmentation of public urban space in the city, through the setback of the plaza of the Seagrams Tower, was the hook for Seagrams to gain a substantial increase in building height. In these examples of deal-making between investors and the city, innovations to the urban context were created by the insertion of alien architecture as a catalyst for new forms of public space. Asset architecture has this potential, but only if not left unregulated.

In the most recent tendencies of asset architecture, the public face of objects with pure urban externality is bounded with an opaque threshold towards a deep architectural interiority, laced and involuted with great intricacy. Urbanism is under threat in this model by the commodification of post-human architectural space, and the remnants of public space is compressed into a visual screen on the external envelopes of extruded footprints. The conception of urbanism in the AAD's projects is limited to infill sites on single manhattan blocks, as a constraint which could benefit from the subversion of urbanism into the exclusivity of its interior architecture. Urban architecture has the power to catalyze and transform its host city. The most ro-bust, if not cliché example of this phenomenon was Frank Gehry's Guggenheim Museum in Bilbao, Spain. Is the Bilbao Effect possible if the public is excluded from entering the interior or a large urban building?

The International Style consolidated architecture as monolithic investment vehicles serving to park and proli-ferate wealth. Super tall pencil towers are today the emblematic typology of asset architecture, limited to small plots and extruded to unprecedented heights for residential buildings. The skyscraper in this accelerated investment model is thus reinvented, yet again. A further speculation of the orientation for this innovation is to exceed the spatial, geometric and material intricacy, or "visual opulence" in Ali Rahim's words, of complex envelopes, is to invert urbanism towards the interiors of these extrusions[12] and to shift the empha-sis of explorations of the complex spatial involutions of these pencil towers towards an interiority which is transgressed and subverted as truly accessible space of the city. John Portman's Bonaventure Hotel in 1976 in Los Angeles was the prototype for the miniaturization of the city in an interior form of urbanism.[13] In this model, city invades the exclusivity of the fortress-like boundary of asset architecture. Rem Koolhaas' provocation in 1994 was to assert how "bigness enlists the generosity of urbanism against the meanness of architecture. Bigness = urbanism vs. architecture"[14] Urbanism must now strike back against the autonomy of asset architecture.

Four Short Stories about Ny-long-kong: Paradigms, Methods & Models[15]

Opportunities created by economic acceleration in these three cities have generated and procured great wealth through investment-led development. Inequity and exclusivity are the worst of the side-effects. Design and Finance are both models of practices aiming to embed intelligence into their methods of engaging with the products of their endeavors. Smartness consolidates associative logics, adaptivity, and customization as methods. These notions are increasingly the basis of the compounding of technology on cities, in which the design repercussions of smart, sentient systems on the city have yet to be adequately explored.

A model of an individual building, or a model as a method of working across a multiplicity of buildingsdoes not record a single instant, but rather, a model in this sense is a mechanic assembly with capacities to yield variants. The repercussions of design processes which can quickly generate multiplicities and serial differentiation bias variation over repetition, and difference over sameness. Models are not blueprints. They have many forms. In fact, models are formless until informed. Plasticity and interactivity drive the shaping of outcomes in the processes and positions argued for the AAD program.[16] Methods which lead to these articulated design outcomes distinguishes the AAD projects as pioneering, set in the context of a post-industrial, informational economy and design environment. The current information revolution has arrived and is rapidly developing. The consequences of Intelligence and automation for individual buildings is becoming clear, yet the potential for the organization and expression of cities of this industrial transition is yet to come.

1. Parametric Urbanism

Cities have always been parametric in the ways in which in that the city is comprised of complex associations and interaction of diverse and numerous agents, systems, and forces. Through deep relationalities between parts to entireties, urbanity achieves dynamism, rather than stasticity, adaptivity rather than fixity and finitude.[17]

Buildings as assets are conventionally produced more via Excel spreadsheets of business plans and pro-jected profits, in relation to regulatory planning and building code parametrics. Hong Kong's pencil towers are extruded houses, whereas Manhattan's pencil towers have larger footprints. Architecture, in this milieu, is the expression of immaterial wealth maximized into three-dimensional matter. It is by these ruthless, market-driven, even simplistic and banal means, that urbanism in the accelerated economies of Ny-lon-kong achieves its legibility and coherence, principally through the economic parameters constraining its architec-ture.[18]

M. Christine Boyer credits Luigi Moretti with initiating the concept "parametric architecture" in 1957, and curating the *Mostra Architettura Parametrica* (Parametric Architecture Exhibition) in Rome, in 1960.[19] Moretti founded the Institute for Mathematical and Operational Research in Urbanism (IRMOU), which experimented with the mathematics of infrastructural flows and the optimization of urban zoning. He wrote that "scientific research, the enumeration oftheparameters, and the quantitative mathematical analysisofthese parameters aretasksthat the new architecture will have to face, in a priori manner in every case. In this way "parametric architecture, as a sentient and sensitive set of processes and products, will be born."[20]

New York, London, and Hong Kong are all engineered and marketed to their free-flowing civic consum-ers, through the most valued criteria: pragmatic, free-market mercantilism. Urbanism pulsates with dynamism and vitality in its everyday real-time, fueled by more than just the density of buildings, it is the intensity of interactions in these cities which are indivisible.[21] It is though, Ny-lon-kong's agility and tenacity to remain profitable which defines the resilience of these cities, but their political power lies in how they can adapt and evolve over time.[22]

2. Adaptive Urbanism

Interior architecture in asset architecture is adaptable within super-tall inflexible structures, with great constraints on preventing alterations of external envelopes. The AAD's methods of computational and material modelling in an interactive design environment seeks to address the indeterminacy of contingencies of adaptive cities, during an important transition to a new industrial paradigm.[23]

In the 1960s, Gordon Pask argued for an evolutionary cybernetic position on urbanism, such that urban change "can be modelled as a self-organizing system and in these terms, it is possible to predict the extent to which the growth of a city will be chaotic or ordered by differentiation."[24] As Mark Burry had declared more recently, "Cities always have cranes sticking out of them. There is no such thing as a completed city."[25]

Contemporary design methods apply evolutionary methods, which cycle through possible options, not simply to determine the best, optimal solution to a problem, but to unleash specific provisional formulations addressing an instant in specific criteria, without making universal claims on propriety and optimal performance. In this light, the city, both understood as its immaterial economy and its material fabric, is always imperfect, unstable, complex, and even wild, in both their behaviors and their forms. As the most complex intricate web of systems humankind has invented, designed, unleashed, cities now require great effort to be controlled. Some complexities and indeterminacies can be modeled, yet the organizational structures of cities are inherently responsive and adaptive and defiant of being predictable.[26] In this dynamic understanding of the behavior of the city, the regime of "free market urbanism" of Ny-lon-kong's tycoon investors, appear as a complex of forces, both controlled and planned, and also somewhat out of control.[27]

3. Customized Urbanism

The prototyping of a differentiated architecture leads to an urbanism biased towardsheterogeneity and difference, rather than sameness as a model of coherence. The AAD program is in fact a prototype for the outcomes of the experimentation on asset architecture. This third short story, or paradigm – can also be articulated as a distinctive urbanism – is conceived through progressing the post-Fordist discourses of late capitalism. What are the repercussions for urbanism of the normalization of computational fabrication and manufacturing? Technology, when applied to the formation of architectural and urban character and identity, escapes culpability for its effacing of traditions. Mass customization has, as a precondition, an inherent pursuit of variation towards differentiation. This particular paradigm has brought forth some admissions about postmodernity, and the ways in which pluralism trumps unity.[28] New York, London and Hong Kong are all post-industrial cities, which share similar legacies of their architecture being mass manufactured. Rem Koolhaas in a lecture at The University of Hong Kong in 2010, declared, "the more boring the buildings, the more coherent a city they make." He was referring to Hong Kong, which in fact, suffers from unrelenting, and rather uninteresting background architecture, yet when read cumulatively, its urbanism is unique and memorable.[29] This view of Hong Kong aligns itself with Koolhaas' argument for the *Generic City*[30] and the *City of Exacerbated Difference*, rather than his earlier championing of New York's high density Manhattanism.

4. Intelligent Urbanism

The basis of any theory of intelligence is rooted in the capacities for feedback and learning. The intelligence of urbanism, different than in discrete buildings is foremost the capacity to achieve the ambitions the three paradigms described above: to apply associative logic towards harnessing urban complexity; to install me-chanisms of adaptive and evolutionary to change into the material fabric of cities; and to yield organizational material variation and specificity at scales between individual buildings, localized districts and entire cities.[31] Smartness in urbanism empowers the fabric of the city with capacities to sense its complexity and dynamism. This sentience is what further substantiates the lifelike qualities of the city, functioning and behaving as an organism, and dismantling, so to speak, the mechanical metaphor of the city.[32]

New York, London and Hong Kong are three cities which are each, in their own ways, frontline battlegrounds of what is prosaically called today, the smart city – between the democratically empowered and informed citizens and the mechanisms of surveillance and authority, all in the name of efficiency, sustainability, and security. The potentials of sentient and augmented urban architecture in this controversial political arena are being prototyped in the projects of the AAD.

Conclusion

In sum, by the time of writing for this third issue in a series of journals, launched by one of the preeminent post-professional graduate programs in architecture, the AAD, focusing on asset architecture as an agenda, there is great benefit in hindsight. The AAD program is researching alternatives to known conventions and professionally executed projects, through engagement with a deeply fraught and complex intersection of architecture, economy, technology, and culture. What has become clear in the body of work of the AAD is the extent to which the unfinished project of the city is at stake. Strategies and tactics of subversion

are possibly preconditions to the maintenance of the status quo of the trajectory of the association of the production of architecture within the flows and accumulations of wealth.

In the post-industrial society in which this work is conceived and executed, the cultural potentials of asset architecture are as much to be explored as the heightened economic context may afford. This contribution to *Asset Architecture 3* argues for public participation in the largely privatized and bounded space of asset architecture. Urban architecture, and hence cities, through architectural aggregation, are all produced and advanced not only by investors, but also, collectively, by its citizens. Governance, it should be maintained, is what stands between the power of capital and the people. Cities, such as New York, and London and Hong Kong, are where some of the pressing social, economic and ecological problems of the twenty-first century lie, but also where opportunities are to be found.[33] Asset architecture may indeed catalyze new formulations of public space and interactivity in the city, but only by the inclusiveness of urbanism winning over the exclusivity of this new, accelerated tendency in the architecture of Ny-lon-kong, asset architecture.

[1] Time Magazine cover, 28 January 2008, © Synapse Group

[2] Rem Koolhaas, *Delirious New York: A Retrospective Manifesto for Manhattan* (Oxford: Oxford University Press, 1978). 128

[3] David Ruy, "Globalization 2.0," *Asset Architecture 1*. Ed. Ali Rahim, (University of Pennsylvania, 2015).

[4] Christopher Hight, "Objectives of Desire," *Asset Architecture 2*. Eds. Ali Rahim, Robert Neumayr, (University of Pennsylvania, 2016).

[5] Colin Rowe, Fred Koetter, *Collage City* (Cambridge: MIT Press, 1978).

[6] Sanford Kwinter, "How I learnt to Stop Worrying Yet Still Not Quite Love the Bomb", *Requiem for the City at the end of the Millennium* (Barcelona: Actar, 2011). 30

[7] Simon Sadler (2000), "Open Ends- The Social Visions of 1960s Non-Planning", *Non-Plan: Essays on Freedom, Participation and Change in Modern Architecture and Urbanism* (Oxford: Architectural Press, 2000).144

[8] Simon Sadler (2000), "Open Ends- The Social Visions of 1960s Non-Planning," *Non-Plan: Essays on Freedom, Participation and Change in Modern Architecture and Urbanism* (Oxford: Architectural Press, 2000).148

[9] Patrik Schumacher, "Free Market Urbanism – Urbanism beyond Planning," *Masterplanning the Adaptive City: Computational Urbanism in the Twenty-first Century* (New York: Routledge, 2013). 237

[10] Donald Trump and Tony Schwartz, *Trump: The Art of the Deal* (New York: Balatine Books, 1987).

[11] David Graham Shane, "Chapter 3, The Metropolis," *Urban Design Since 1945 – A Global Perspective* (London: Wiley, 2011).88

[12] Ali Rahim, "On Aesthetics," *Asset Architecture 1* (University of Pennsylvania, 2015). 33

[13] Jonathan D. Solomon, "Hong Kong – Aformal Urbanism," *Shaping the City: Studies in History, Theory and Urban Design*. Eds. Rodolphe El-Khoury, Edwards Robbins, (New York: Routledge, 2013).109

[14] Rem Koolhaas, "Bigness," *SMLXL*, (New York: Monacelli Press, 1995). 515

[15] Tom Verebes, *UrbanISMS: Paradigmatic Practices and their Multifarious Platforms*, PhD dissertation, RMIT, Melbourne, Australia, 2017 p.219-325

[16] Tom Verebes, *UrbanISMS: Paradigmatic Practices and their Multifarious Platforms*, PhD dissertation, RMIT, Melbourne, Australia, 2017 p.226

[17] Tom Verebes, *Masterplanning the Adaptive City: Computational Urbanism in the Twenty-first Century* (New York: Routledge, 2013). 180-1

[18] Tom Verebes, "Hong Kong: Appearing Dense but Growing Smarter", *Growing Compact: Urban Form, Density, Sustainability*. Eds. Philip Joo Hwa Bay & Steffen Lehmann (New York: Routledge, 2017). 257

[19] Christine M. Boyer, "On Modelling Complexity and Urban Form," *AD Mass Customised Cities*, Guest Ed. Tom Verebes, Profile 138 (London: Wiley, 2015).

[20] Luigi Moretti, "Form as Structure," *Luigi Moretti: Works and Writings*. Eds. Federico Bucci, Mario Mulazzani (New York: Princeton Architectural Press, 2002) . 183-4

[21] Justyna Karakiewicz, Tom Kvan, Barry Shelton, *The Making of Hong Kong: From Vertical to Volumetric* (New York: Routledge, 2011). 16

[22] Tom Verebes, "Hong Kong: Appearing Dense but Growing Smarter," *Growing Compact: Urban Form, Density, Sustainability*. Eds. Philip Joo Hwa Bay and Steffen Lehmann (New York: Routledge, 2017). 258

[23] Tom Verebes, "The Interactive Urban Model: Histories and Legacies Related to Prototyping the Twenty-First Century City," *Frontiers in Digital Humanities, Digital Architecture*. Ed. Jeffrey Huangm, 2016 http://journal.frontiersin.org/article/10.3389/fdigh.2016.00001/full

[24] Gordon Pask, "The Architectural Relevance of Cybernetics," *Cyber Reader: Critical Writings for the Digital Era*. ed. Neil Spiller (London: Phaidon, 2002). 79

[25] Donald Bates, "Permanence and Change: An interview with Mark Burry," *Architectural Design*, Mass Customised Cities issue, Guest Ed. Tom Verebes (London: Wiley, 2015). 82

[26] Tom Verebes, "Hong Kong: Appearing Dense but Growing Smarter," *Growing Compact: Urban Form, Density, Sustainability*. Eds. Philip Joo Hwa Bay and Steffen Lehmann (New York: Routledge, 2017). 259

[27] Patrik Schumacher, "Free Market Urbanism – Urbanism beyond Planning," *Masterplanning the Adaptive City: Computational Urbanism in the Twenty-first Century* (New York: Routledge, 2013). 132

[28] Tom Verebes, *UrbanISMS: Paradigmatic Practices and their Multifarious Platforms*, PhD dissertation, RMIT, Melbourne, Australia, 2017 p.335

[29] Tom Verebes, *UrbanISMS: Paradigmatic Practices and their Multifarious Platforms*, PhD dissertation, RMIT, Melbourne, Australia, 2017 p.283

[30] Rem Koolhaas, "The Generic City," *SMLXL*, (New York: Monacelli Press, 1995). 1248-1264

[31] Tom Verebes, "Hong Kong: Appearing Dense but Growing Smarter," *Growing Compact: Urban Form, Density, Sustainability*. Eds. Philip Joo Hwa Bay and Steffen Lehmann (New York: Routledge, 2017). 268

[32] Tom Verebes, "Hong Kong: Appearing Dense but Growing Smarter," *Growing Compact: Urban Form, Density, Sustainability*. Eds. Philip Joo Hwa Bay and Steffen Lehmann (New York: Routledge, 2017). 255

[33] Tom Verebes, "Hong Kong: Appearing Dense but Growing Smarter," *Growing Compact: Urban Form, Density, Sustainability*. Eds. Philip Joo Hwa Bay and Steffen Lehmann (New York: Routledge, 2017). 254

DETAIL SECTION MODEL: INVISIBLE TOWER - ALI TABATABAIE GHOMI, YUCHI WANG, MEARI KIM

STUDENT WORK: ASSET ARCHITECTURE STUDIO

ALI RAHIM, ROBERT NEUMAYR, NATHAN HUME, EZIO BLASETTI

In the historical development of Manhattan, ever since the grid was laid over its territory, architecture, due to its ability to increase land value through densification and building mass, has been a generator and expression of capital. To multiply inhabitable area, the city's architecture incorporated and stacked the city's land area in towers. From the beginning of the twentieth century, the skyscraper, as this typology came to be called, became an expression of commerse through built form, incorporating the whole city under one roof. Today, the tallest towers in the city go far beyond these earlier expressions of capital to serve as assets in and of themselves, developed and sold as monetary instruments for global investment. We call this asset architecture.

In the fall 2016 MSD-Advanced Architectural Design studio, students took a critical approach to such asset architecture, developing designs for new pencil towers in Manhattan. The shared sites for the studio projects were all seven pencil tower sites in Manhattan, 225 West 57th Street, 36 Central Park South, 157 West 57th Street, 111 West 57th Street, 220 Central Park South, 53 West 53 and 432 Park Avenue. Some of these towers are in their planning stages and others are under construction.

As it was the third and final year of the design research, students addressed the challenges of the studio in a variety of ways including explorations of the potential of asset architecture to offer novel hybridized spaces to benefit the surrounding city. Projects combined residential space with vertical parks, wedding halls, charter schools, a veritical cemetary, a megachurch. Some viewed asset architecture itself as a precious object, creating high-rises that function to frame coveted views of the surrounding city as well as for the curation, preservation, and collection of fine art. What are the limits and potentials of asset architecture? How far can the concept be pushed and how can it be reconfigured and reintegrated into the fabric of the city? One project even goes so far as to suggest that asset architecture can function as valuable infrastructure for the city's dead by designing a mauseleum in the center of Manhattan.

Understanding architecture purely as a means of generating capital, the projects developed in the studio speculate on how the architecture of the city of New York might increase its asset value by fusing urban elements into a new form of architectural interiority. Together they demonstrate that Manhattan is uniquely suited for translating asset architecture into proposals that could make unprecedented links between architecture, global investment, and Manhattan – the financial capital of the world.

SPEEDTRADER

POWERED BY GREEN ENERGY TO OPTIMIZE EFFICIENCY, SPEED TRADER SETS A NEW STANDARD FOR HIGH FREQUENCY DATA CENTERS BY OFFERING TRADERS THE FASTEST EXECUTION SPEEDS. DESIGNED TO MAXIMIZE PROFITS FROM HIGH-SPEED TRADING, THIS TOWER LEVERAGES ITS PROXIMITY TO INFRASTRUCTURE AND FINANCIAL INSTITUTIONS TO REDUCE DATA TRANSFER DELAYS.

ANDRES DANIEL CELY, TIANYI SUN, YUHAN BIAN

JURY DISCUSSION

Rahim: So Mathew, let me put you on the spot. What do you think of the frequency of trading as an asset?

Soules: It's interesting. Are you asking in terms of its form?

Rahim: In terms of its relevance...to make $250 million more potentially because of its location.

Soules: It facilitates the trades.

Rahim: The form is, like Daniel said very clearly, an instrument to provide the infrastructure to accommodate high-speed frequency trading closer to Wall Street.

Soules: It is intelligent on your part to put forth the argument for a new vertical condition in Manhattan that takes us back to things like the AT&T tower, a kind of new avatar of this hyper device. I think it's smart. One thing I am interested in is how you think of these buildings beyond generating height profits through a kind of instrumentality that goes above and beyond the architecture itself. You found a program that embodies an instrumental role in increasing profits. My question is once you generated that opportunity for yourself, what is it about the materialization of this and the presence of this program that adds value beyond the facilitating of high-speed trading. So I want to know how do we understand this not in in terms of its role in finance but in its more sculptural nature. I think this is interesting. How would you respond to that?

Student: I think Manhattan is losing a huge opportunity by not doing this at a larger scale. There are lots of data centers in Mid-Town but they are all moving to New Jersey, so most of the companies and traders that were on Wall Street are moving to Jersey and they are all working in small rental office spaces. A huge and interesting population is

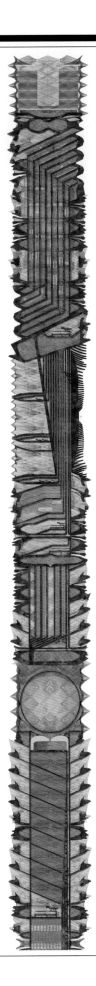

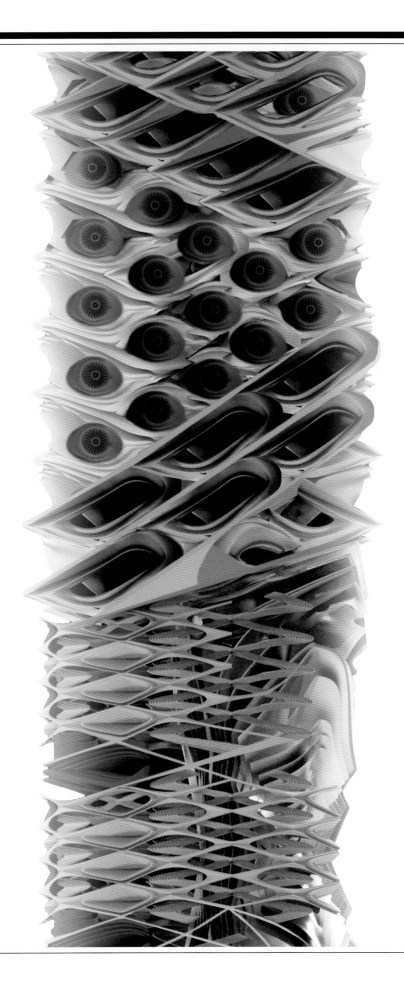

Student: moving out of New York, and they will probably start living in New Jersey soon if we do not think about providing this type of infrastructure in the city. I like to compare this to 432 Park Avenue. This building is the same size but actually has double the usable surface. The other one is housing and of course it produces a lot of revenue, but this one could produce double that if we simply think about area. As a mayor of the city I would promote this type of investment to concentrate money in Manhattan, I would not want investors to leave the city. About the community, I am sure the neighborhood will start to change a lot just for being next to this building.

Cohen: What about the form? You are very good at explaining the scenario. But what did you think about the form?

Student: For the exterior we tried to use the downdraught effect as a natural cooling system, creating a facade that has this directionality to pull the wind to the interior as much as we can.

Cohen: Why is it differentiated two-thirds up?

Student: Because the neighboring tower makes the wind different at this level. This was determined through a very simple analysis in EcoTect.

Cohen: So the form is a result of a rational response?

Student: Yes, and no. There also multiple moments where we wanted to explore formally. The interior is rational while the exterior is also about creating something special for the city, something that people would enjoy. That would be my way of thinking.

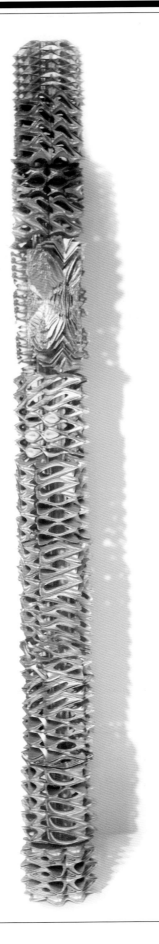

"THIS IS REALLY A
MONUMENT TO THE
WHOLE WORLD OF
INVESTMENT TRADING
AND THE MARKETS
THAT THEY UNDERPIN.
IT IS VERY MUCH A
MONUMENT TO SHOW
THE IMPORTANCE
AND EMINENCE
OF INFORMATION
TECHNOLOGIES TODAY."
TOM VEREBES

Cohen: Well that's great, but all of your colleagues did that too. That is too general. Those kinds of generalizations would cover 90 percent of the winds in the world. They don't really get to the essence of this particular building.

Kolatan: When we look at this sort of design we can have a discussion about cities in terms of their neo-liberal qualities and that kind of fame and asset urbanism. It seems like there are two ways to frame this in this context: one would be as a form of resistance and the other would be acceleration. I think it's absolutely relevant, not just as related to this particular project, but as it appears that all of them, to me, these are acceleration projects rather than projects of resistance. Then the question becomes at what point do we accelerate? Are you comfortable with accelerating it to a level of aesthetic excess, or do you actually propose an acceleration beyond that actually would undermine the asset quality that is being generated in the first place? This is more than a cultural question and I am not expecting an answer to that but that is one of the questions that I am pondering by looking at all the projects together. It has to be super articulated, super expensive and super like this because it accelerates the argument, completely outside the functional argument.

Dubbeldam: Architecture becomes an important investment tool. So on that level you could say there is unlimited money to build this.

Kolatan: Is this a model of the future for New York or are we showing this as a current condition?

Dubbeldam: In this case, he is talking about investments.

Student: All of us are currently investing in the internet, Facebook, Google, the cloud, etc. all these webpages have data centers somewhere else that we never get to know, and actually this is getting now out of the field of architecture and its becoming engineering. I think we should not lose this in the cities, people should get to know how these thing work.

Kolatan: Then this is the right question to ask; are you really trying to make it a performative, functional argument? If so, I don't think you could carry it through.

Verebes: Not with a data center, since data centers are almost like fortresses. Such buildings made of super thick concrete walls to resist whatever could happen. They are designed to last a long time and to keep people out. They are usually anonymous, generic and do not express visual or memorable characteristics. Everything is opposite of what you have done. you may have built a model that is super porous, a building that you could see entirely through, but I think the intention was to kind of create an atmosphere of openness and super articulation rather than something really closed and generic. I think in some sense the type of poetics that you are raising is that this is really a monument to the whole world of investment trading and the markets that they underpin. And it's very much a monument to show the importance and eminence of information technologies today. To build a tower in Manhattan like this would be the ultimate monumentality of the information society

Massey: But it might be that by foregrounding and branding something that usually remains backgrounded and by making that operation precarious and vulnerable, that it might harbor some of those acceleration tendencies that Ferda is pointing to and that potentially destabilizes the function of Manhattan as a financial center. It seems to me if there is a critical potential in this project it might be in setting up the conditions of failure. It quite possibly becomes the number one terrorist target in the U.S., quite vulnerable to disruption because of its porosity.

Rahim: It's not really porous.

Student: Exactly. Each of the openings in the facade corresponds to what's going on inside

Cohen: What to do you mean by accelerationism?

Massey: It is an idea that by intensifying the evolution of capitalism you destabilize it and trigger a crisis that pushes you into some new condition.

Cohen: Outside of this building, let's say the acceleration could be symbolic, programmatic, financial. I think there are a number of ways that could possibly accelerate but these are what cause the form, I would argue in this case.

Kolatan: Is the argument that because we are in this sort of constantly getting faster, neoliberal capitalistic society, what can we do? The acceleration argument says that actually there is absolutely nothing we can do but we can further push all these tendencies until they come to a moment of breakdown. That's the only one.

Cohen: I might say that the first tower we saw today, the one by Shop, is exactly that.

Soules:	I don't agree at all. I think one of the qualities I see in this project is the impossibility of tenant improvement, to change over time. You can't reconfigure the interior. Sometimes intensifying jams the machinery, so there is a way that I think these buildings will fail rapidly. Probably a market failure since the specificity of the market that produces it is not meant to last.
Massey:	There is a question that architectural decisions are intervening in the potential political economy of architecture.
Cohen:	I think that there are versions of acceleration that only serve neo-liberal capital and there are versions of acceleration that gets so intense that they shift, they become something else. So it seems to me that many of the projects do not accelerate to the point where they shift. In my critical assessment of the studio you could say they are actually neo-liberal. To go back to Manhattan in death capitalizes on opportunities of using existing information to speculate, to leverage debt and power to re-cast it to something else. It's certainly neo-liberal logic, something material, formal, and programmatic. It could be any form. There is no form that corresponds to it. It could have adopted to the language of Viñoly. Why does it not work?
Student:	The cooling systems would work with that.
Cohen:	You don't think for example, maybe Renzo Piano, the early work? I mean, could you solve it technically and manifest the technical solution with the instruments rather than a form like this? Why couldn't the formalism be manifested by the machinery itself? The structure would support the machinery. Would this be adequate? Why do you have to introduce these surfaces?
Student:	I like to think of this building as a car design. You have machinery inside which might be very powerful and you have all the conditions to make it work perfectly, but then, if you have a form that works with that it will help the machinery work more efficiently. It's like comparing two cars with the same engine but different forms, one would be more efficient than the other.
Cohen:	I like your argument, I just wish you were more rigorous about it. I mean, if you would show me how this form does it.
Douglis:	It is interesting that most of the comments address the rest of the projects, and this is an anomaly. I would argue this is probably the first infrastructural project in the studio and that Jonathan's comments take something of such enormous influence and importance from a technological standpoint for the city and reduce it to the singularity of one building. This is conceptually a fraud. I would argue that this is the one project in the studio is a multiplicity. The infrastructure, which is initially understood to be very horizontal, now moves up and occupies the domain that is typically allocated for living and to the extent that it does, then the question is would you reveal it, does it declares itself like a monument, or does is function in a much more sinister way where there is a series of skins that don't reveal its interiority and its intentionality. I think this is a loaded project and its quite projective and in a context where most of the projects where unaware of that hyper indulgence that actually anticipates their own demise. If we take the design issue of the table on this one, I think the programmatic diagram has an enormous opportunity as a conceptual model to think about new infrastructure projects in the 22nd century.

COMBINING ELEMENTS FROM BROWNSTONES AND SKYSCRAPERS, SKYHOUSE IS FORMED BY TWISTING, MULTILEVEL UNITS THAT OFFER 360-DEGREE VIEWS. THIS HIGHRISE HYBRIDIZES THESE TWO TYPOLOGIES TO PRODUCE UNIQUE LIVING SPACES. IT'S NOVEL FAÇADE FEATURES FEATHER-LIKE POCKETS AND GAPS TO CREATE SINGULAR SPACES AND INTERIOR LIGHTING EFFECTS.

BOQUN HUAI, YUE PENG, HEWEN JIANG

SKYHOUSE

JURY DISCUSSION

Douglis: The ambiguity or the multiplicity between the indoors and outdoors is what you're positing. The language of the façade falls somewhere in between a claw and animal hair in the sense that it begins to peel away and light and air are able to penetrate into the building. The project is much more sophisticated in terms of understanding the syntactical language of the proposal, and having essentially extended into three dimensionally into the x,y, and z directions. There is a clear schism between what is being proposed about the façade and its inability to penetrate and integrate in a more graceful and elegant way into the plans and sections. The program is brilliant and you have to be clear about what the brownstone offers you. The fact of the front stair, the setback, is both an object or device of transition and the circulation but it's also furniture. It's activated as a sort of public living room. The arrangement of the public and the private is also interesting. Some of these qualities of brownstones are shown in the diagram of the plan, not in the language of the architecture.

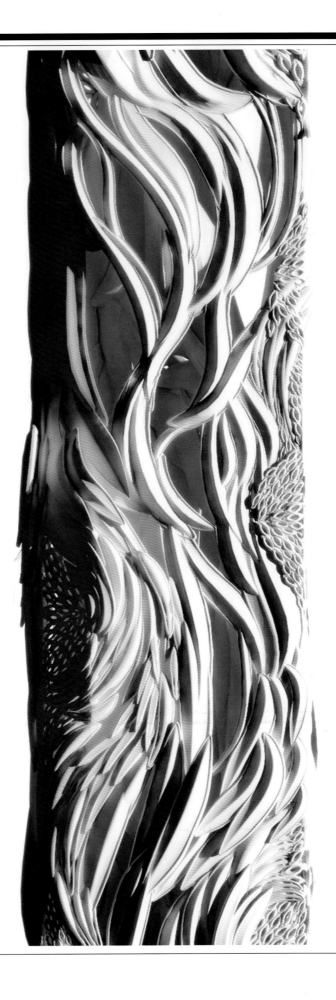

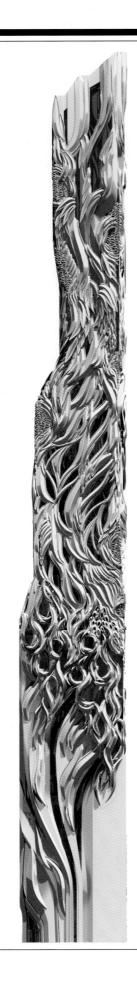

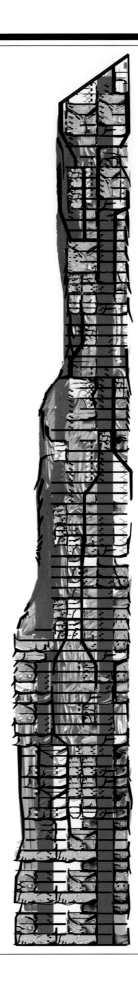

"THE LANGUAGE OF THE
FAÇADE FALLS INTO
THE AMBIGUITY AND
MULTIPLICITY BETWEEN THE
INDOORS AND OUTDOORS. IT
BEGINS TO PEEL AWAY AND
LIGHT AND AIR ARE ABLE
TO PENETRATE INTO THE
BUILDING. "
EVAN DOUGLIS

HEPHAESTUS

HEPHAESTUS FEATURES VERTICALLY ARRAYED SHARED WORKSPACES FOR ENTREPRENEURS, FREELANCERS, AND STARTUPS, A FLEXIBLE "WEWORK" TOWER DESIGNED TO MEET THE EVER-INCREASING DEMAND FOR TEMPORARY OFFICE SPACE IN MANHATTAN. SPACES ARE DESIGNED TO MEET INDIVIDUAL NEEDS AND APPEAL TO DIFFERENT TYPES OF USERS, FROM FREELANCERS TO STARTUPS.

SHUOQI XIONG, KAI TANG, JIA LYU

Verebes: This project could be anything, and it could be reduced down to a comparison to the SHoP Architects' tower at 111 West 57th Street. It could be a SHoP Architects' facade. Just in comparison to that infrastructural project that seems to argue that its expression is less connected, here it is almost so disconnected that it could be arbitrary relative to some of the other projects. I like that it's not another binary project. But it really seems that there is an arbitrary method to the facade. I am much more interested in this kind of seamlessness between interior and exterior expression of the final project. There seems to be a way in which the volumes of the interior and exterior play out. It is beautiful. The simplicity of that envelope as it becomes rounded on the corners and at other times creates big open spaces, this project has a deep articulation and yet still some vast spaces. There is something quite restrained, and yet some discussion about exuberance. The strength of this project is that it has to have tall and big open spaces in the interior. This is probably one of the first projects that does that.

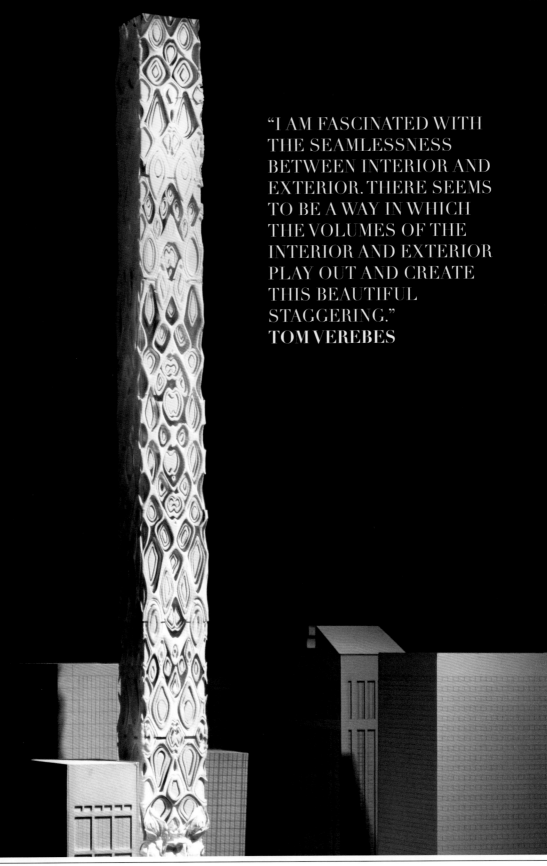

"I AM FASCINATED WITH THE SEAMLESSNESS BETWEEN INTERIOR AND EXTERIOR. THERE SEEMS TO BE A WAY IN WHICH THE VOLUMES OF THE INTERIOR AND EXTERIOR PLAY OUT AND CREATE THIS BEAUTIFUL STAGGERING."
TOM VEREBES

CELEBRATING ROCOCO ORNAMENTATION, VERSACE TOWER CREATES LIVING SPACES THAT STAND OUT AS WORKS OF ART. THIS TOWER WAS DESIGNED TO COMMUNICATE THE ESSENCE OF CAPITALISM THROUGH AN EMPHASIS ON TRANSPARENCY AND REFLECTIVE SURFACES THAT PRODUCE DIFFERENT QUALITIES OF LIGHT.

XI CHEN, FANGJIE GUO, YIJIA WANG

VERSACE TOWER

Kolatan: What I think is critical in all of these projects is that they seem to so aggressively over articulate on the formal level. To me this reading makes particular sense within the asset argument since it is not only a programmatic shape—what towers usually do—but It's also an expression of a system that is based on acceleration. Looking like that I see very different buildings, and I think that's why it makes sense to me, even though it is literally a Rococo building.

Soules: We didn't really talk much about Versace tower, but I've spent a lot of time writing about and studying Sullivan and other architects. The Versace is interesting because it's the one that is least naive about the capacity of nature to have a new form. Like Versace, I am going to muster a time-honored signifier of wealth and status, that is almost kitsch at this point, and find something in that. I appreciate the different sensibility here and don't necessarily prefer one over the other. But it stands out differently.

Jamelle: It is symbolic and almost political at this point. This is a good point where architects can intervene, so that it's not cynicism.

Soules: I just want to recognize the question of cynicism and accelerationism, that open-endedness is apparently optimistic.

SECTION

DETAILED SECTION
DRAWING

ELEVATION

DETAILED ELEVATION
DRAWING

OVERALL VIEW
OF THE PHYSICAL
MODEL

DETAIL VIEWS
OF THE PHYSICAL
MODEL

"IT IS THE LEAST NAIVE ABOUT THE CAPACITY OF NATURE TO HAVE A NEW FORM—SIGNIFIER OF WEALTH AND STATUS THAT IS ALMOST KITSCH. THIS OPEN-ENDEDNESS IS APPARENTLY OPTIMISTIC."
MATTHEW SOULES

KALEIDOSCOPE TOWER CREATES A NEW CENTER THAT WILL ENABLE MOMA TO EXPAND ITS STORAGE CAPACITY WHILE ALSO OFFERING SPACE FOR PRIVATE ART GALLERIES AS WELL AS TRADING AND AUCTION ACTIVITIES. USING THE CONTEMPORARY ART MARKET AS AN ATTRACTOR, THE TOWER WILL ALSO SERVE AS AN INVESTMENT OPPORTUNITY FOR WEALTHY INDIVIDUALS, COLLECTORS, AND ART-RELATED ORGANIZATIONS.

XIAOYU MA, JIEPING WAN, KAIKANG SHEN

KALEIDOSCOPE TOWER

JURY DISCUSSION

Soules: What can one see as the relationship between the ground and the height, the diversion of towers that changes across their vertical length? There is something about its skin that provokes that question in my mind more than the others, the incredible abstractness, that you can flip it around and you can move it.

Kolatan: You mean in that sense it's still very modern?

Soules: Yes, and I mean incredibly abstract in this way.

Kolatan: That's what I mean, that the notion of the abstract tower as one of the main paradigms in modernity.

Soules: And it meets the ground exceptionally elegantly.

Verebes: When one looks at the plans, there is a depth that comes into view. There are these elements that have such different depths and they are so extreme in how big they are at some levels. They look like the curtain wall in some of these, but in others, just huge bone-like pieces. It's that it repeats itself and it doesn't go through a transformation that is relative to where it is in the building, so it just keeps repeating. But there are some absolutely stunning moments where the corners are incredible, absolutely beautiful, and I would have loved you to have expanded a little bit the theory of different light that come through.

Massey: It would be so much more interesting as a small building in some ways because it seems like the language of this monolith could be turned into a pattern instead of a particular form, and each of these are themselves like their own entities if they overlap a bit.

Kolatan: I have to say, given the critique, which I think is a dilemma of high rise buildings now, making something really tall remains somewhat in the realm of possibility, but could express a more dynamic formalism. So to me all of them in that sense are some kind of compromise. This one still relies on a level of repetition, and I think it does it really quite beautifully. I have to say the longer I look at this the more I like it. I see more and more how the corners have been worked out. At one point I look at it here and I go to the top of your model and it continuously changes. And there actually is not a single moment of repetitive form. I know that's very difficult to do so I really appreciate that.

Jamelle: I agree with you. It's more clear from the drawing how the dematerialization really becomes intense in the middle and then begins to reorganize itself. Even though this is a model I find this degree of detail compelling. But I think you needed just a bit more time to do a few more things, one of which is that there is a regularity to this section and the floors and that the experiences with what are happening in the building have no relationship to what I just discussed in terms of the dematerialization at the corners and at the wall and then an intensity of openness. And then it can dematerialize again as it moves towards the base. I think you could benefit from a closer study of the auction experience so you know how to begin to allow that kind of variation, that packing of the auction house. Because if you look at your section you have the same amount of density, all the way through, whereas you would want to see that correlation working with your program in an even more one-to-one way. The section helps to allow the dematerialization. You agree?

Verebes: Yes, in fact it's dematerialized because it's all the same, the same color, the same material. But when you start to read the different layers that are so much more coherent here. If you would have used a color 3D printer to either have transformations along some of these filaments, or the different ones that are layered with different coloration, then it wouldn't have flattened out in the same way.

Cohen: I think the way the model was built is maybe betraying you. You can't cut it like that horizontally. You're going to have to find a way to make the model in smaller parts that conceal the seam. A flower could never have had seams like that. That's too bad because it's beautiful. The rendering is far more persuasive.

"THE CORNERS HAVE BEEN
WORKED OUT SO MUCH
THAT WHEN I SEE TOWARDS
THE TOP OF YOUR MODEL
IT CONTINUOUSLY
CHANGES —
I APPRECIATE THAT THERE
IS NOT A SINGLE MOMENT
OF REPETITIOUS FORM."
FERDA KOLATAN

NESTED MORPH

NESTED MORPH STANDS OUT IN THE CITY, OFFERING A SINGULAR AESTHETIC PRODUCED BY A RICHLY OVERLAPPING, LAYERED FAÇADE THAT PRODUCES AN ATMOSPHERE OF LIGHT AND SHADOWS. THE BUILDING BRINGS NEW IMMERSIVE ENTERTAINMENT SPACES TO THE CITY. ONE UNIQUE ASPECT OF THE TOWER IS THAT INVESTORS CAN PURCHASE INDIVIDUALIZED AND SPECIFIC FORMS THAT MAKE UP THE NOVEL FAÇADE. SIMILAR TO HOW VIEWS OF CENTRAL PARK CAN INCREASE ADJACENT PROPERTY VALUES, THESE EXTERIOR ELEMENTS ARE ENVISIONED AS WAYS TO GENERATE OPPORTUNITIES TO INCREASE THE PROPERTY VALUES OF ADJACENT BUILDINGS THAT HAVE VIEWS OF THEM. THE TOWER THUS FUNCTIONS AS AN ECONOMIC CATALYST IN THE CITY.

SIYANG LV, CAN WANG, YUCHEN ZHAO, SOOKWAN AHN

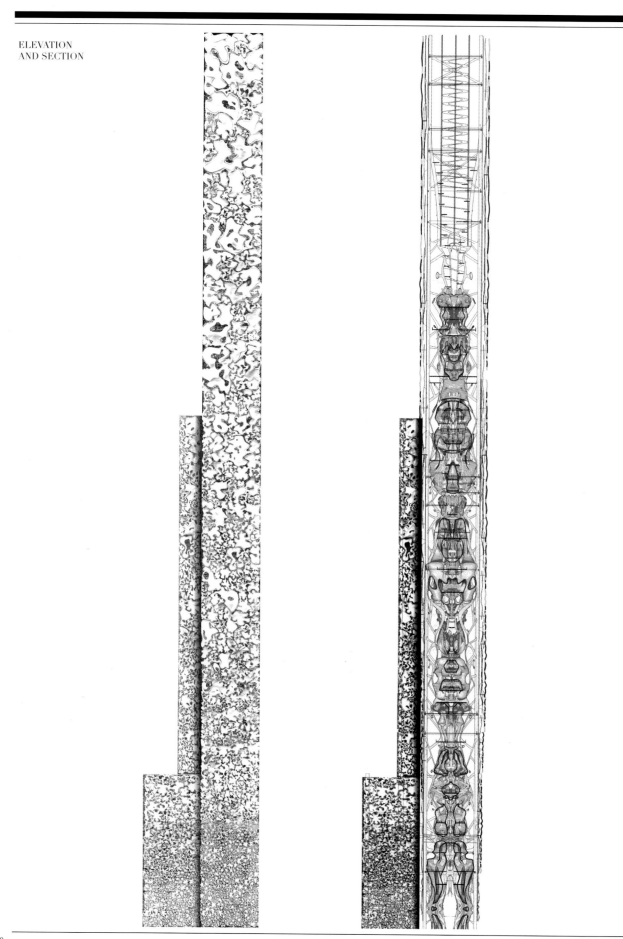

Soules: I find the section of this one particularly compelling because of the way its stacked and voluptuous volumes are relatively small in scale. One thing I find intriguing about this, from a more observationist view, is the way it grapples with this question of opacity in relation to the degrees of inhabitation. I think putting these dark spaces in these ghost towers is an intriguing conceptual move. And, also, I almost want to read the scale as hundred-person spaces, almost as condominium units in a way. So, the luxury units are very large in scale. I'm also intrigued by the notion of what program can be pulled along with the big condo. I find that conceptually very intriguing about the project.

Cohen: The other issue would be the sculptural form of the tower, these voids are limited by the necessity to maintain the planarity of the tower. You could have handled the emergence of the space from the outside. The pure form permits it. I would like to see many types of interiors and different kinds performances. They might be significantly different. You might be able to see a pile of very different kinds of theaters. Maybe some are larger. The shape allows the interior to be read from the outside.

Massey: You could probably bring in the pocket from the exteriority, then you could do something much more interesting.

Cohen: I think you can keep the theater as large as possible, you're already unlimited. Do those voids go under the theater? under the ceiling? Above the acoustical ceiling? Obviously, you should've used the voids and theaters, exactly where they are, under or on top. All I'm saying is the skin of the building conformed itself around the body, so it doesn't have to be true.

Douglis: Maybe the collective assertion of the studio is that architecture is soon going to limit the site and it's going to extend that, and then there is a dialectic between what's inside and outside. The plans, section, and interior are so extraordinary. To me, with all due respect, it's totally absurd to bury it in a bar building, in a tower. It's crazy. You have two choices: one is to rip the facade off and let the sky be an enormous sculptural organicism of the theater vessels, so that profile of the building is the theater-stacked profile. The second option, which is a slight variation, is to say there is no facade—the portion of the structural system is moved out to the corners and there is a secondary program that meanders. In other words, we have a theater district at central park, moving up the vertical axis—hybridized multi-purpose program. You have outdoor space and indoor space. You have two different types of theater: one is entirely virtual in terms of what takes place, filmless as an example. The other one is this beautiful colossal playscape that is about meandering around the geometries, which is absolutely fantastic.

Soules: I think there is a very powerful argument about the relative small scale of these theaters and their size is proximate to luxury condominiums. I think the project could be far more conceptually rigid and fascinating if these theaters were condominiums and units. In other words, people can use them while they can also use and be employed in the theater. So there would be a double-function.

Cohen: It's radical. You use it as an apartment, or use it for your own theatrical decadence. It's not purely acting as a theater. I don't think the infrastructure is big enough on the plan. They are too tiny and there are too many of them. That's why they needed the double-function. Otherwise, there should be less theaters and more housing here. I think you should permit double-function.

Douglis: We have to remind ourselves that we see these as successful business models if you display the novelty of the architecture. The novelty is on interior, not the exterior.

Jamelle: Do you want to build a theater anyone will know next to your theater, even though the teathers are distributed? You also have all the noise, the crowds, the number of flat billboards? One of them is not flat. The boards are not for sale, but they could be cellular. They could become spatial. They could become inhabitable units. Right now, you are showing it just as a skin. And if they become flat, these roofs can be clouds you could puff through the building. That could lead the way to different scales. If you are seeing this from far away, you see these suspended theaters. You know quite well what they are. What if these become spatial? They become apartments. Let's see retail. What if they were stores?. Big stores. But in doing that, you have a new type of theater, you have a dynamic experience. I like it very much. I like the section very much. All these are experiences.

Massey: If, just like the Sullivan tower, some of these rough theater bladders intersected the façade, the geometries could be comfortable and you could reach a little to the exterior.

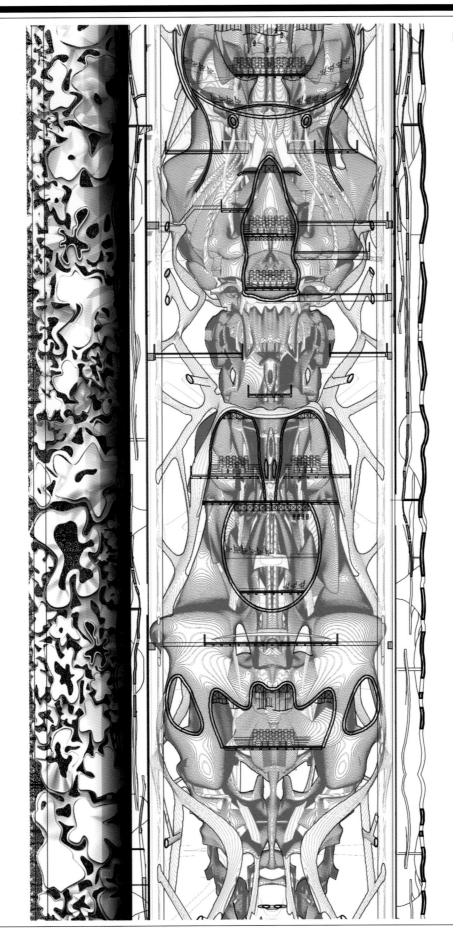

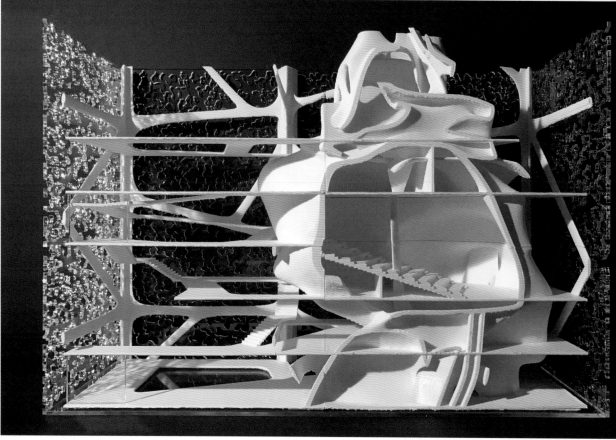

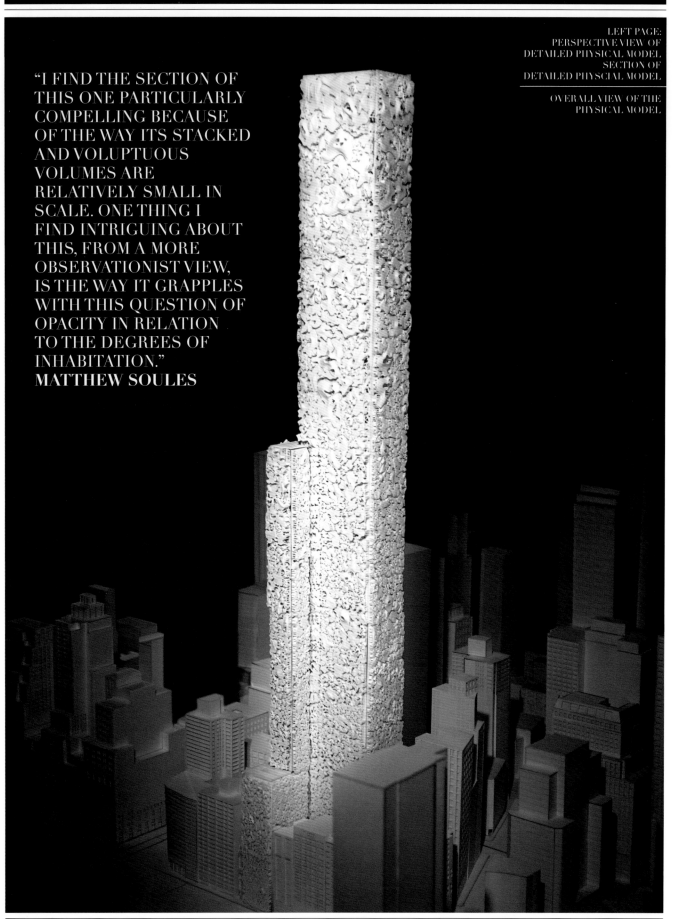

"I FIND THE SECTION OF THIS ONE PARTICULARLY COMPELLING BECAUSE OF THE WAY ITS STACKED AND VOLUPTUOUS VOLUMES ARE RELATIVELY SMALL IN SCALE. ONE THING I FIND INTRIGUING ABOUT THIS, FROM A MORE OBSERVATIONIST VIEW, IS THE WAY IT GRAPPLES WITH THIS QUESTION OF OPACITY IN RELATION TO THE DEGREES OF INHABITATION."
MATTHEW SOULES

LEFT PAGE:
PERSPECTIVE VIEW OF
DETAILED PHYSICAL MODEL
SECTION OF
DETAILED PHYSICAL MODEL

OVERALL VIEW OF THE
PHYSICAL MODEL

ONE MILLION TOWER

A MILLION INVESTORS CONTRIBUTE TO A MILLION PARTS TO PRODUCE A TOWER THAT SERVES AS A NEW PUBLIC AMENITY, A VERTICAL "CENTRAL PARK". ONE MILLION TOWER STANDS AS AN EXPRESSION OF SPATIAL CROWDSOURCING, GENERATING UNIQUE INVESTMENT OPPORTUNITIES AND ATMOSPHERES.

JIANBAO ZHONG, MENGYUE WU, XIAONAN CHEN

"ALL THE EFFECTS ARE GENERATED HERE BY TAKING THE NOTION OF ORNAMENTATION AND USING THAT IN A SCULPTED AND BEAUTIFUL WAY TO DEVELOP THE FACADE."
FERDA KOLATAN

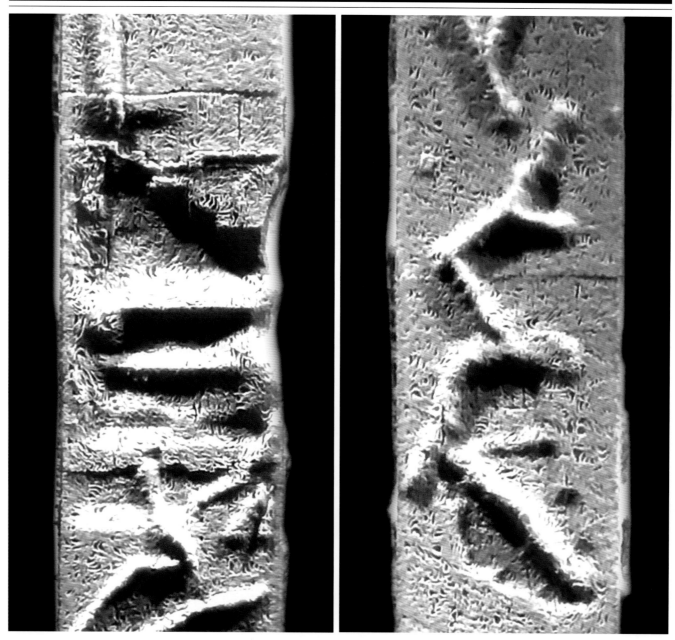

JURY DISCUSSION

Kolatan: What I really like about this project is that it has a really cool skin. It's really fantastic. All the effects are generated here by taking the notion of ornamentation and using that in a sculpted and beautiful way to develop the facade. To me it resonates with the past. Also, just in terms how you are designing these elements, it seems that it is way more ambiguous and I personally appreciate that. I also appreciate the way structural elements begin to work together with the parts that are non-structural and feathery. The only critique at this point in terms of the exterior is that there is also a certain homogeneity. It's basically repetitive. Each one of these are qualitatively exactly the same.

Soules: But it seems to me that you are using structure in a certain financial way. Let's say that a typical condominium of this volume and scale would have 200 or 300 investors. You want to produce thousands by itemizing incremental value at the level of the skin, which is super fascinating. I wish they would consider that more intensely from the performative standpoint. This one works innovation into the interior and structure. As a totem, right? The exterior acts as a communicative device to produce desire on the part of investors. It embodies a relationship to investors that is fascinating. What is it about these topologies, the ruffles? They facilitate a relationship that is fundamentally different than 432 Park Avenue or any of these other pencil towers. I think the question relates to heterogeneity, diversity, and the perforation of difference across the surface. The degree to which this is repetitive might undermine what you are seeking. I think you could push this notion to their topology.

Jamelle: If you consider this as structural, this would've been a more important connection point. Where these particular veins are coming out of these pieces could begin to tell you how the substructural elements work with the façade. This would be a beautiful project, rather than having these horrible horizontal pieces. But, the fineness, thinness, how it drapes, with the structure—what if that was all transparent? And then this would been some other material that is attached to the glazing. What I am trying to say is that it would have been interesting if you pushed how to think about the transparency. What if these were transparent in places rather than opaque?

Verebes: I think it's not just the opening size or base. I totally agree with you. The seams are potentially jigsaw puzzle-like rather than a series of rectangles. But also the base expresses such weight and thickness. You also have this skin for the core where you have a fire separation and the seam. All of these elements would bring light into the floors.

Soules: Every tower has structure and mechanical systems, but I'm not sure your thesis is about that. You're presenting your idea as an investment opportunity. So I don't care about structure. You have this specific skin, which is pretty fascinating, and there is a reason for this in your thesis. You can just say, "This is just a cool tower where we are going to investigate a whole set of issues and there are many amazing things about it." Can you answer how you see this relationship between this new idea of investment and this tower? We can talk about structure. We can talk about windows. But how do you answer that?

Douglis: All these financial models are only successful if the architecture is able to produce an enormous amount of attraction in terms of monolithic seduction. On a micro level, there is an enormous amount of novelty and variation that is taking place. Maybe, if you wanted a paradigm shift, there is a history of windows they've got right. This beautiful calligraphic meandering, almost like a biological proposition, begins to expand and contract in the XYZ axes. And you would have to do a tremendous amount of work to make this perform structurally, or to handle the wind loads. There is a whole series of intentionality that could be invented in this. Where it's having great difficulty at this point is the lighting. Unlike 95 percent of the projects in the studio, it's going to have great difficulty performing at a distance. In other words, the porosity is subtle and obsessive at a local level. There is enormous abundance of lines that laminate through it to create this colossal hollow condition. That is a contribution to architecture. To the extent that it has to assume the monumentality of a skyscraper, I think you have two choices here. So, there is this whole conversation about climate, when you illuminate the interior, which is an intent to try to figure out how to create some form of variation from a distance in the skyline. One is that it goes totally stealth. Or it's totally illuminated. It is the most subtle and iconic tower in the city, with no variation at the larger scale. Or, it somehow exercises the potentiality of the local, introducing gyration or wobble into the skin and move this extruded plan. In other words, the thing starts to have an angst built into it to exercise something new out of the local. To me, it still resides within this ambivalent phase. It's beautiful (cut out) and It seems to me to be not only designing a large-scale building in elevation, but also designing it from the street level perspective. There is an understanding and recognition that there are optical conditions that need to be accounted for in the topology, ornamentation, and scalar variation, so that certain sensations are acquired in the process. From the ground level—and we haven't spoken about this—this would be the one project where, in order to reinterpret historical precedent in a contemporary way, you would be able to find a whole series of interesting things that would be fundamentally different and more ambitious than we're currently capable of.

Cohen: I think the initial impulse to look for a material solution is the first thing that really struck me about this. However, I don't think you can suspend belief quite so much. I understand you can suspend the engineering question. I'm blocked 95 percent, compared to Shop which is completely transparent. You need to build in that question immediately and think of ways to address it. How do you link this appearance and negotiate an interior experience? For all of the conversation we've had on the asset nature of the building, it has to have a view. What happens if it doesn't? Maybe not at the lower level, by the way. It suggests to me that, interestingly enough, that it is a questionable assumption that we walk in the city. It is not what we often do. But if we do do this, you could have opacity at the bottom. It might have been a virtue that the building is more introverted at the lower floors. Comparatively, the bottom is meant to be a facade.

THE ABYSS

THE ABYSS, IS THE AGGREGATION OF VERTICALLY MAXIMIZED MICRO-UNITS TO PRODUCE PERSONAL SKYSCRAPERS FOR TENANTS. THESE NOVEL MULTI-STOREY UNITS ARE STACKED TO OFFER RESIDENTS A UNIQUE SPATIAL EXPERIENCE THAT EMPHASIZES A CATHEDRAL-LIKE VAULTED QUALITY WITHIN A REDUCED FOOTPRINT. THEY ALSO EMPHASIZE AN EXCLUSIVE, PERSONALIZED QUALITY THROUGH PRIVATE ACCESS.

ANGELIKI TZIFA, KE LIU, DONGLIANG LI

JURY DISCUSSION

Kolatan: The elephant in the room is the language of form that we have not been talking about all day, which is fairly consistent throughout the studio. I think, actually, the project on the mortuary was different somewhat, and there is one that had the vertical elements on the façade. But all of you are invested in a sort of organicist formal language. I don't know the reason but it has to do with him. But I think in this case, if these spaces had been represented without any geometry, just to understand the potential of what you are talking about, just the vertical shafts and the shelves, I think you would have learned something about the process of making these new types. You would have learned it more clearly than being mesmerized by the confusion caused by these forms. They are in the way, obstacles to be looked at. I don't know why you need it. About 25 percent of the plane in consumed by the movement of surfaces.

Douglis: Scott, I hear you but I am uncomfortable generalizing about the studio because it sounds like Patrik Schumacher when he does parametrisism and he takes all these beautiful diversities of schools of thought and he puts them under one umbrella. But let's get off that one. Two hours ago you were talking about absurdity.

Cohen: Every project is about understanding what a tower can be.

Douglis: Let me finish. So, let's assume that there is a disproportional manner of exuberance and density in relation to program and use. Might the projects be at a point where you could prove or you could perform a kind of autopsy that in a certain degree or ratio would have taken place and that some of that utility could be reclaimed?

Cohen: But why don't we talk about what the form does for us but also the virtues in the formal language? I am not saying that the formal language is without virtues. I just want to discuss it. I am not saying to eliminate the formal language. I just want to understand what it is doing. I think in this particular case it might not be helpful, but broadly it has been.

Jamelle: It's a great idea. It might be underdeveloped? But is there a potential for a new way of looking at compact living? Yes. And that's what they are after.

Cohen: Yes, but they are confiscating it too much.

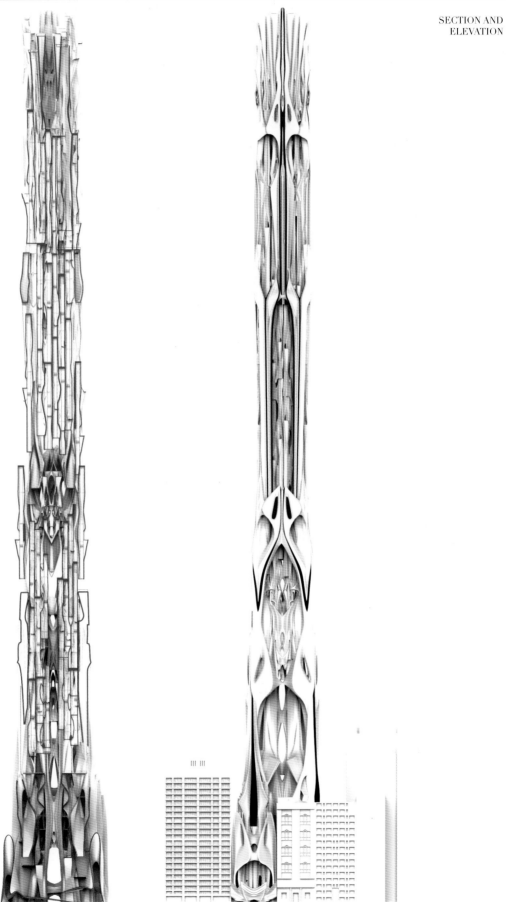

DETAILED SECTION DRAWING

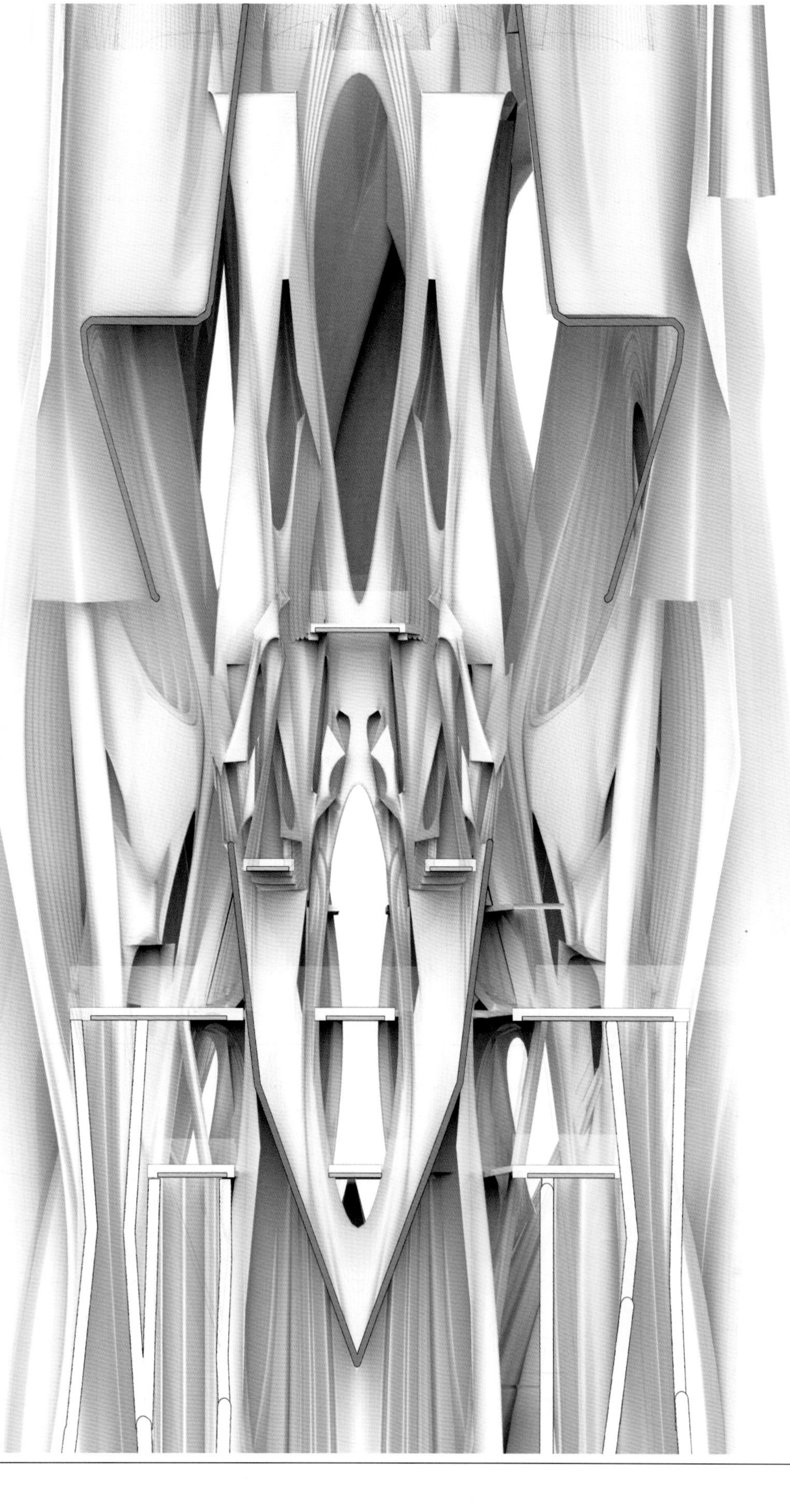

Douglis:	We have to agree that we don't have an engineer and there aren't a series of experts that can help to address this to a higher degree with specificity. But I would argue that the colossal nostrils of the elevation of the building have an enormous amount of potential.
Cohen:	What would you do with it?
Douglis:	What would I do with nostrils? I want to figure out how it participates in terms of the physics of building, to be honest with you. At the same time, there might be a series of co-interest in terms of program use, morphology, and the technology of the building. I cannot address that because I don't think that was a priority for them.
Cohen:	It doesn't seem related to the elevator.
Douglis:	No I agree with you. I think there is too much density at the top. It is like a city of flutes. These things are stacked along the vertical axis, and I think what you were talking about, which is important, is how you penetrate the flutes and make areas of expansion and contraction. In other words, can the residential spaces begin to acquire more realism.
Cohen:	One thing about compactness is the opportunity to inhabit these kinds of unusually formed spaces, where you inhabit these crevices, where all your artifacts of life can be stuffed into the dense poche. I think there is an opportunity there to rotate, to have the plan look something like that. I think the plan is more convincing than the elevation. I like when you call it fluting, because flutes generally extrude in a way which can be much more consistent. Whether they taper or not.
Douglis:	This would be a great project in Tokyo, where culturally there is a collective understanding that you will require a small and limited amount of space for domesticity.
Cohen:	The other thing that is exciting about this is the brilliant kind of implication it has on the elevator issue, which we haven't talked about today. How long would it take to bring people to a unit? How big do the cores need to get to serve a tower this tall and to make it possible? The whole question is what the elevator does in a building with such a small footprint that is so tall. So what you've done is fascinating. You make the units themselves take on this problem where they are inherently part of the whole system of the elevator. I think it is a great idea to take the whole idea to get rid of the core as an independent entity, in a way. You are criticizing it, at least you are trying a new way. That's great.
Soules:	I think it is also incredibly fascinating in relation to the dominate trajectories of luxury living, to have your own individual elevator that runs into all these problems surrounding the individual, isolated footprint of the building, to make the building out of hundreds of individual elevators with micro-distances that you then travel laterally from one to another. I think this is fascinating. To go back to your original comment, I think what is missing here is a greater exploration of how these lateral cross-tube movements occur.
Cohen:	Crossing from one vertical to another.
Soules:	So I think that wants to happen in a multiplicity of ways. It is a kind of beehive of crossovers from tube to tube and I think you want to be able to see how you explore it in plan and section.
Cohen:	I think the plan could absorb plumbing and other systems. The plan looks like it is already thinking this way. The whole elevation on the left is a manifestation of a system of interlocking elevators.
Jamelle:	What you value in an apartment is the least amount of circulation. Circulation is the most wasted space. Everyone desires that every single unit has no circulation. Here, there is no circulation in the building. You tested the boundaries of the too narrow. It is a great project. But it needs to be resolved so we can understand the inhabitability of some of these units. But I think developing it will make the project better not worse. The plan of the ground floor reminds me of a plan like a cathedral. And that is what it takes up from this kind of fluting, the grandiose structure of the debarring skin. And the plan of a cathedral. That is really something.
Douglis:	Of course you can design more, but there is a different type of drawing that they can make because one of the innovations here is that the houses are distributed in the vertical axis and we don't understand the branch logic in plans and the sections. It is a three-dimensional proposition. So, you could get six views of the city. Your house is elongated as a piece of rubber, but you don't pick it up in these projections.

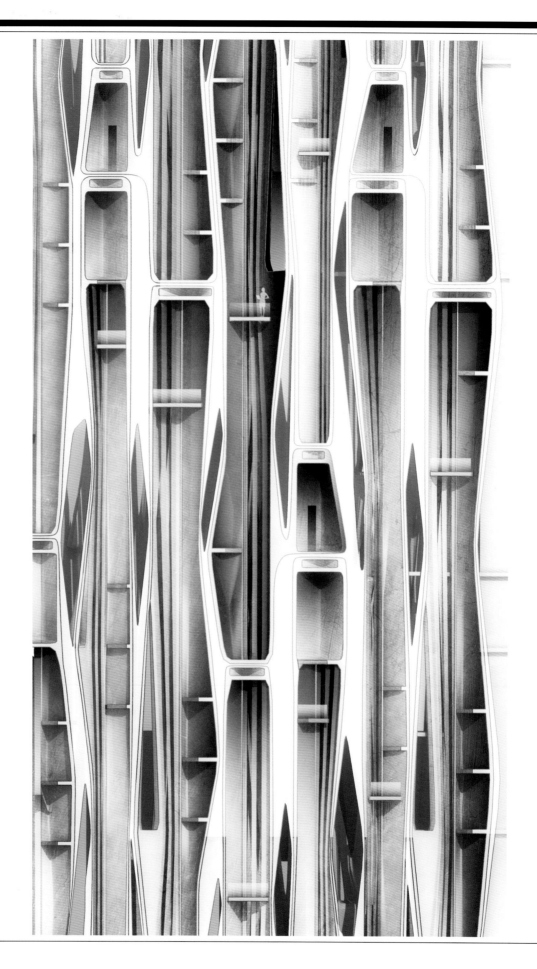

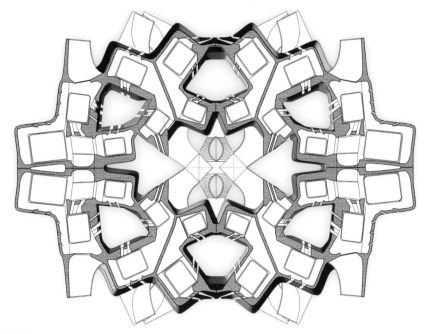

LEVEL 1

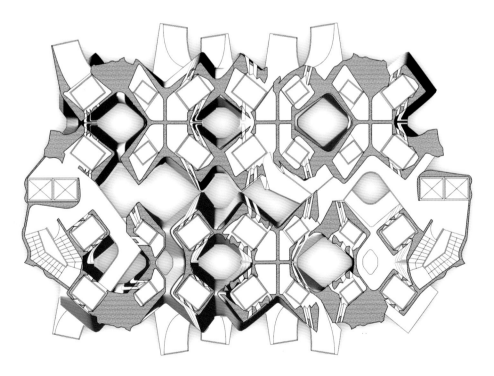

LEVEL 2

PERSPECTIVE VIEW

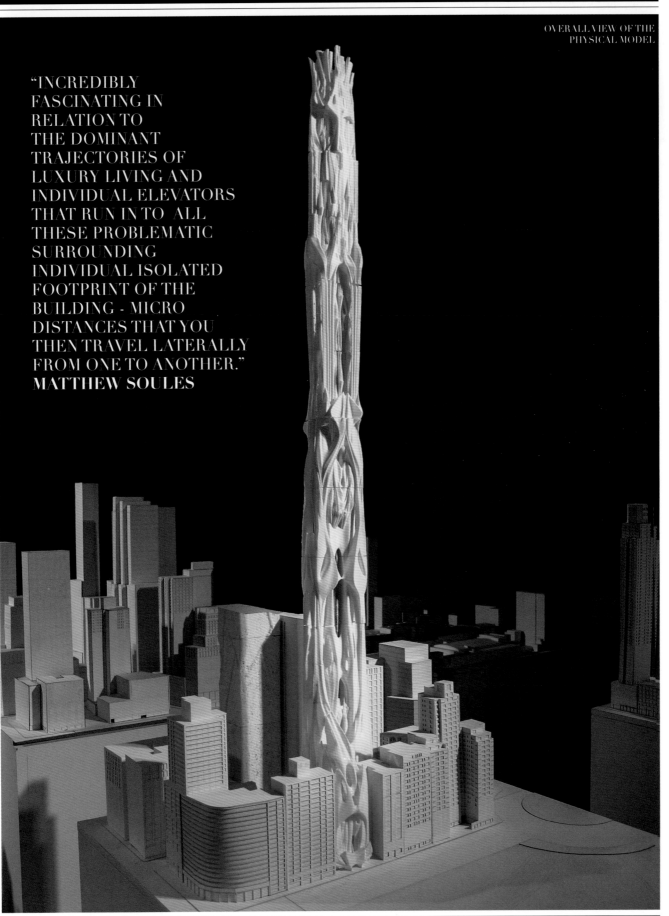

"INCREDIBLY
FASCINATING IN
RELATION TO
THE DOMINANT
TRAJECTORIES OF
LUXURY LIVING AND
INDIVIDUAL ELEVATORS
THAT RUN INTO ALL
THESE PROBLEMATIC
SURROUNDING
INDIVIDUAL ISOLATED
FOOTPRINT OF THE
BUILDING - MICRO
DISTANCES THAT YOU
THEN TRAVEL LATERALLY
FROM ONE TO ANOTHER."
MATTHEW SOULES

PLOUTO

MADE UP OF VORTICES TO HOUSE FINE ART AUCTION HOUSES AND GALLERIES, PLOUTO IS DESIGNED TO TAKE ADVANTAGE OF ITS ADJACENCY TO MOMA TO SERVE AS A NEW HUB FOR THE GLOBAL ART MARKET. THE TOWER TRANSFORMS FROM ITS "L" SHAPED BASE TO A RECTANGULAR PLAN AS IT INCREASES IN HEIGHT. THREE DISTINCT TYPES OF VORTICES REPRESENT DIFFERENT FUNCTIONS. THE CENTRAL VORTEX SERVES AS AN AUCTION HOUSE. THE SECOND TYPE, THE SUB-VORTEX, HOUSES EXHIBITION SPACE. THE THIRD TYPE, THE CORNER VORTEX, IS FOR OFFICE SPACE.

XUECHUAN QIN, CE LI, JINGYI SUN

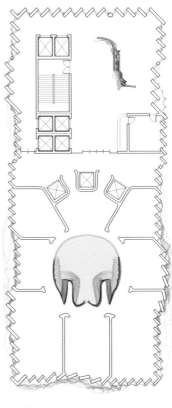

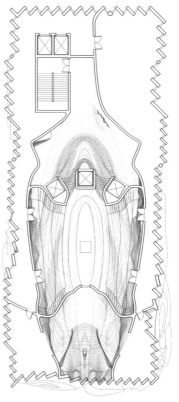

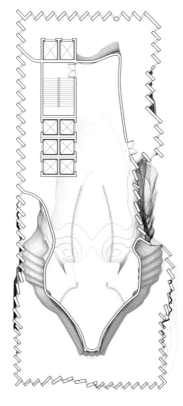

LEVEL 1   LEVEL 2   LEVEL 3

Kolatan: It's interesting to me that this project is much more like the singular gesture. It looks more like a weather pattern or something you usually see more in horizontal design, a kind of flow that has been folded and framed. So, in that sense there's absolutely zero repetition. But because it finds itself so expressed in the frame of a tower I feel like it's more conventional in that sense. It's an interesting juxtaposition.

Soules: In a similar fashion, I really want to see this milled out of a single piece of timber, instead of veneer with evident seams.

Cohen: Again, you can hide those seams if you add a complicated dovetail and you would have to make that part of the project. But the seam itself is part of the project and that will help you discover the little moments. Given that you're speculating, the model itself becomes the work. In the middle of so much fiction, maybe the model could be the only reality in the project and you could accept it to some degree as being evidence of some encounter with fabrication.

Jamelle: This one is more compelling because it goes off with the different coloration and also the chunks of wood. Maybe it's better from far away but this one, to me, is more mesmerizing. I do ask the same question here though. I like your plans. I like the 41st floor plan, it's really great. I like how the exhibition halls turn into the auction room. It would be a really great experience to be on one of those floors. The 41st floor is strong but I don't see how, where it begins to tornado more, what's happening here? It's a beautiful model but here you're expecting this vortex but it's the least interesting part of the model. You really want to put it together in terms of where the auction room is and where the common meeting area is. You expect a crescendo, so use it.

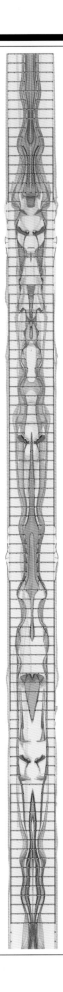

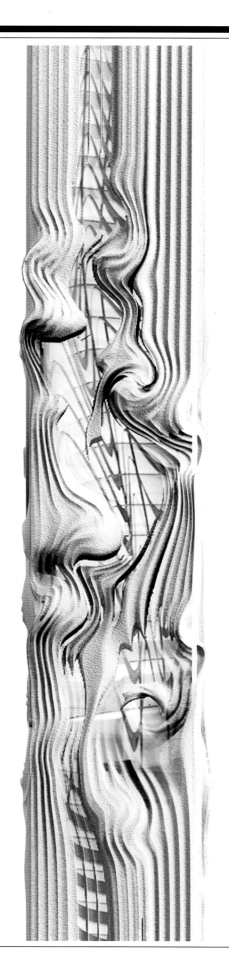

"THE WAY IN WHICH
THE EXHIBITION HALLS
TURN INTO THE AUCTION
ROOM FORMS A GREAT
EXPERIENCE. IT IS A
BEAUTIFUL MODEL."
HINA JAMELLE

TO MEET THE INCREASING DEMAND FOR CEMETERY SPACE
IN MANHATTAN, VERTICAL MAUSOLEUM IS A NEW TYPE OF
SKYSCRAPER. THE TOWER OFFERS MULTI-DENOMINATIONAL,
MULTICULTURAL FUNERARY SERVICES TO APPEAL TO PEOPLE
FROM A MULTITUDE OF BACKGROUNDS. ITS STRATIFIED
FAÇADE SERVES AS BOTH SUPERSTRUCTURAL EXOSKELETON
AND VERTICAL CEMETERY OR MAUSOLEUM SPACE, WITH
BURIAL SPACE LOCATED UNDERGROUND. VISITORS ARE
LEAD THROUGH THE BUILDING THROUGH THE SYMBOLIC
TRANSITION FROM SPACES OF DARKNESS TO LIGHT.

BOSUNG JEON, CARRIE FRATTALI, XIAOYU ZHAO

VERTICAL MAUSOLEUM

Douglis: It's great to see a financial model whether its 100 percent accurate or not. We can't judge, but I really appreciate the fact that you are making a financial case linked to some of the architectural strategies.

Soules: I think insofar as a financial fiction that can be offered as a space at this review, I think it's really quite plausible. You're building is remarkably plausible in my opinion. What is a rich form of engagement in relation to questions of creating realism and? I think your project really occupies a rich and exciting space that has that tension, pushing things far beyond the status quo. It's very projective but it taps into this sort of realism; it's very rich in that way. I think that also relates to a fairly straight forward—in a good way—adoption of human rituals around death. You haven't sought new typologies of that but you've sought to adhere existing practices of worship and recast them in a vertical form. I think it's quite intelligent and rich and I think it's a super fascinating project. Even the exterior, the way it harkens to a verticality one finds in religious spaces. It's got anorgan-like feeling. There's all of these open significations that have to do with accepted rituals around death and mourning and celebration that it encapsulates, but it also doesn't open in a generous way. It's not a lavish reproduction of these forms and its really smart.

Cohen: It's a very convincing alternative. The character of the interior seems to be strangely and peculiarly hitting a very interesting point. Almost fantastical. Almost the iconography of *Star Wars*. It has a mid-century modern restraint combined with that. We can't deny something else super important here. That there's this brilliant transcendent condition of being up high and so elevated. Something about a thing that is normally so grounded and the opacity in the air, the nation of the earthy and the transcendent. I find it very convincing. You could write quite extensively about this. We should be more specific about the critique and how you get into designing the actuality. I would have many studies of the aggregation of these spaces. And in this case, Evan and Matt, who earlier were saying to suspend reality, and for the first time we will suspend reality because the whole premise is so intelligent. It's the correct scale and opacity. How do you make a building with an exterior that has and enjoys opacity? There are so many reasons it works. It opens up the whole question of speculation. You can do a whole studio on a mausoleum tower.

Massey: Where are the lakes and parks? And I don't necessarily mean that they will be actual lakes and parks, but one of the market premises for the cemetery that you're citing is variety of neighborhoods and landscape features that are distinctive and that create hierarchies of value. I don't know that you've created this. There's a high degree of formal consistency once you get into the project. It's nice but it might go against your business model. And the only thing is whenever I've gone to a crematorium there's a high degree of personalization. Some of that is in the fixed architecture of the plot of the memorial and some of it is in all the things people had. I sense that there is a consistency to the formal language that is working against the market model. I wonder if this same project could accommodate architecturally and experientially different neighborhoods and if it could accommodate the participatory design that essentially happens in existing cemeteries so that I don't have to have a niche identical to every other. I can have my own special niche that expresses my personality and death.

Verebes: I mean there is already a niche variety. You don't get a cookie cutter like everybody else. I want to echo the thought that it's a beautifully worked out project and formalization. As a business model I have a slightly different take on this. Just in the sense, I've lived in Hong Kong where there is huge land pressure and very few horizontal cemeteries that are not historical. Some are up on hills and most are towers. One of the things that they do as an effect is that they create an incredibly negative set of effects financially on everything around it. Anybody with a view of this building could see their property value drop. Perhaps many people in the room would understand the fact that no one wants to look at a cemetery. It's bad luck. The idea that you go to a cemetery to walk around is a very western notion, that you would look at the green spaces and the lakes like it's actually a nice place to be. My simple understanding is that no one want to see them in Asia. They block out windows that look over cemeteries. So there's something about the financial model that in fact might present some negative effects for some people. You create a gross difference of those that wouldn't be bothered by this and some who would find it deeply troubling.

Jamelle: Well that's why you're not seeing any one identifiable object on this facade. I think it's an abstraction of it. There's a shrouding of it. You don't see a park. You don't see any of the smaller scales of the urn, the coffin, the mausoleum, of the ceremonial holes. You don't have any indication of what's going on. It's the least transparent of buildings for that purpose. It's like seeing a picture of a loved one even though they're gone. It comes with that sort of association.

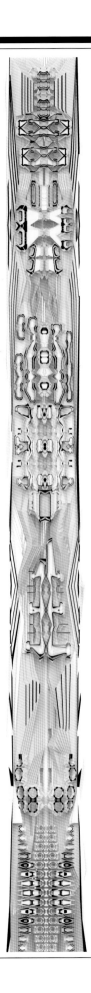

RIGHT PAGE:
PERSPECTIVE VIEW
OF SECTION DRAWING

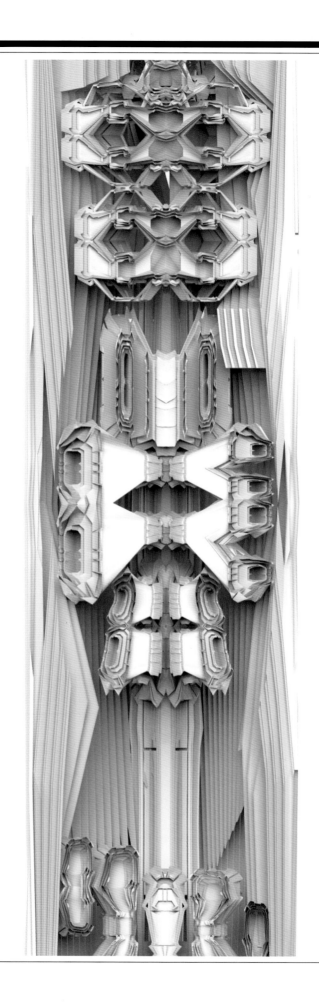

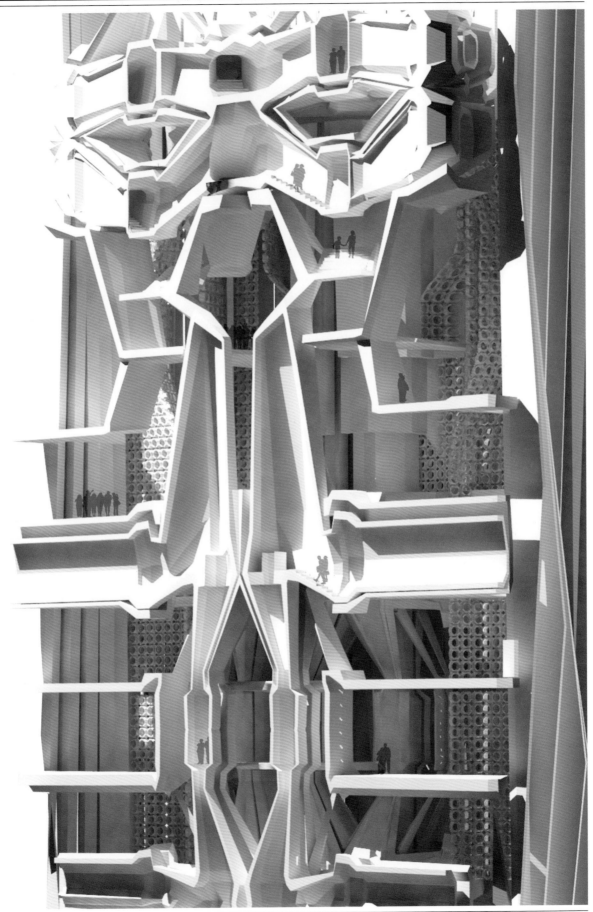

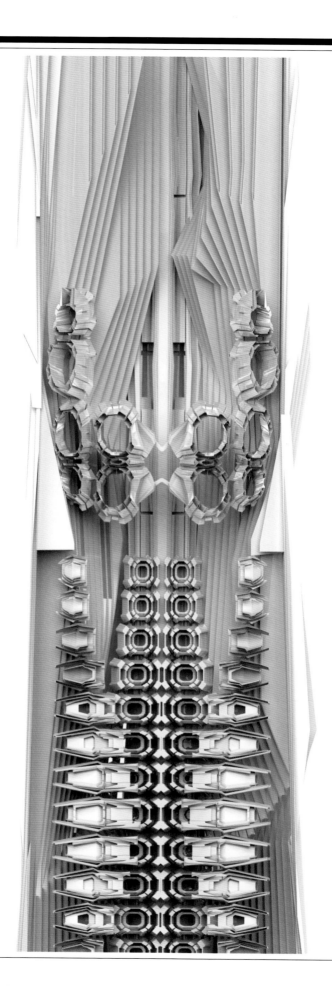

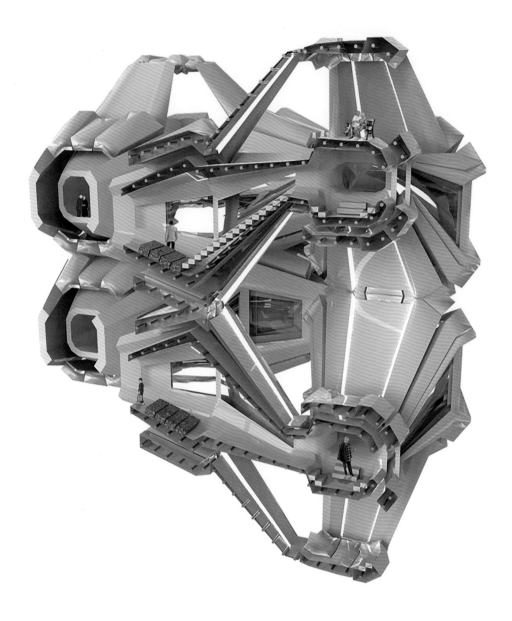

Kolatan: It disappears in some ways. It never would reflect it, would never have backlight. It's the opposite of a building that has advertising all over it. It would completely be camouflaged into the sky and always take on a sort of coloration and visuality of the sky. It's an interesting problem: how to make a building disappear.

Soules: It's an interesting point you raise. The way in which its rendered. There's almost this literalness to its play on this notion of the ghost, the ghost tower. It is specter-like and it has this sort of darkness, this phantom reality. I think the question of its relationship to light and color and, in a strange way, geometry in terms of the perspective, is very important in how you want to imagine cities. So, culturally part of the city, in a holistic way. I find it incredibly beautiful. A really compelling study on how you can play this line to be dignified in some way but then to be open to all the readings.

Cohen: You find yourself in the air just utterly with no program and windswept. It's fantastic as a retreat and as a reprieve.

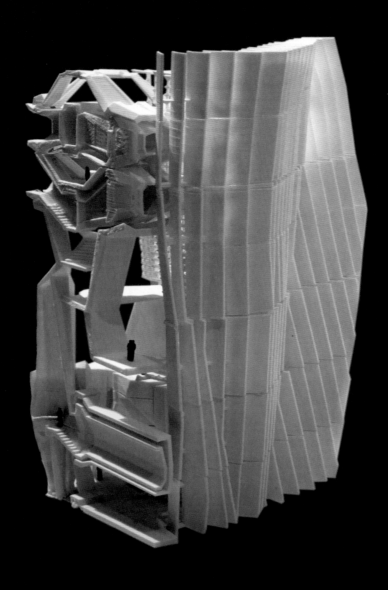

LEVEL 1

LEVEL 2

"THE CHARACTER OF
THE INTERIOR SEEMS
STRANGELY AND
PECULIARLY HITTING A
VERY INTERESTING POINT
WHERE THE TRANSCENDENT
CONDITION IS ELEVATED
HIGH AS OPPOSED TO
MORATORIUM THAT IS
TYPICALLY GROUNDED. I
FIND IT VERY CONVINCING."
PRESTON SCOTT COHEN

ONE VENTURE CAPITAL

DESIGNED TO FUNCTION AS A DISTINCTIVE LANDMARK WITHIN A CONTEXT DOMINATED BY GOTHIC STYLE ARCHITECTURE, ONE VENTURE CAPITAL BRINGS INVESTORS AND STARTUPS TOGETHER TO TELLTHE STORY OF CAPITAL THROUGH DESIGN. ACTING AS AN ICONIC AND PROTECTIVEVAULTED WALL, THE FAÇADE IS COMPRISED OF VARIED OPENINGS THAT REPRESENT DISTINCT INVESTMENTS AND PROGRAM.

TAESEO PARK, MUSAB MOHAMMAD, XIAOYI GAO

Douglis: I'm not an engineer and am most certainly trying to catch you guys because I think it's a spectacular project. Talk about being positive and optimistic. But to the extent that the physics of this type of tower have to come to some reconciliation. To me that represents some kind of new ground rather than discovery of the argument. In your particular case, the figuration of those pass-throughs for the wind load represent an opportunity. It would be important to know when you would see a certain kind of utility as it moves into realm of absurdity. That's not to say that you could still have a huge amount of property and space here for you to get the pass-through and still be a component of the fluidity in the plan and section you want to build.

Cohen: It isn't that it looks exciting from the point of view of speculation. It seems the limits are the reasons that then determine how far you can go. Can you push the engineering?

Douglis: If I understand that correctly, there is a synchronicity and this is a direct correspondence. I actually love the façade. There is something within that makes the logic of that surface, which made it into structure rather than into a distribution model in terms of ownership. I would argue that you need a different set of representational drawings in order to explain it better. Because the model cannot explain the logic clearly, but if you did the drawings these relationships would just speak themselves out.

Jamelle: There is a need for a 3D model or some kind of section because of the relationship between the two parts, the skin and the section. This is one relationship. The other is the skin and these voids, which you are arguing has two rules: one is where the offices occur and another is for the venture capital firm as a group which would almost seem like voids. But if you trying to stitch them up, I like the different layers but none of these have interactions and conversations. So the structure of the skin, the skin and the voids, the voids and the program, within which there are cells. I like the idea of cells and the way these cells are organized with different spaces positioned around them, which I would identify as neighborhoods.

Douglis: It's more complicated than that. It doesn't have to be a clear delineation of the constructive ornaments. It seems to be the typology of that surface in terms of making diagrid striations which represent novel form and I keep looking inside here and trying to understand here how they transition from the normative floor slab, which can be occupied by the space, to the curvilinear dynamism of the cell. There might be something within the evolutionary

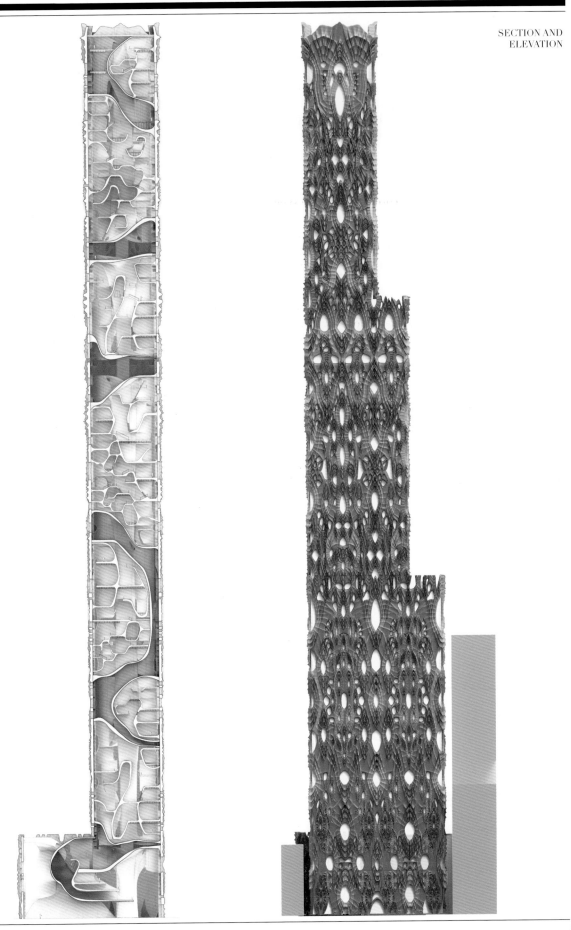

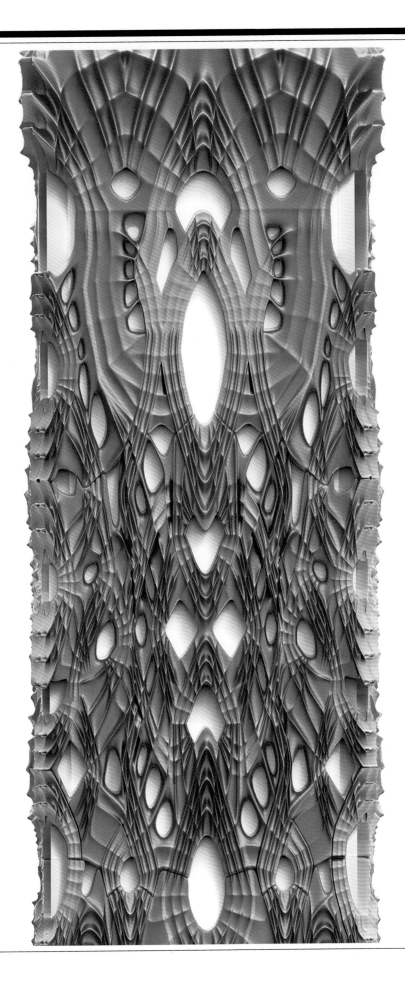

"THERE IS SOMETHING
WITHIN THE
EVOLUTIONARY
TRANSITION FROM
THE SURFACE OF
THE BUILDING INTO
THE SECTION OF THE
BUILDING WHERE
THE FORCE REQUIRES
DIFFERENT AMOUNT
INTELLIGENCE."
EVAN DOUGLIS

Douglis: transition from the surface of the building into the section of the building where you can now require different amounts of intelligence. They build from retinal graphics to something that deals with the physics of a building that is holding itself up. And then it goes to a beautiful space that can be read as amnesia. I'm talking about the performative projects here.

Kolatan: I really like the exterior condition of the envelop. It's very gothic. To me it's very much in the context of the traditional New York, 1920-30s architecture, all the way up and to the top. I don't know if its Intuitive or deliberated by you, but you should really check that out. It makes it almost a contextual project. If I look quickly around, this is the one that is clearly saying it belongs to New York and not to Shanghai or another city. I find it's interesting. But I think it's a little bit strange that you deal with the setback based on the exteriority and quality. The steps are suddenly cut in an awkward way, particularly the first one. The second one is a bit better from where I stand. Maybe it's different from the other side but it seems it doesn't go far enough into understanding how the setback is generating the very important opportunity of the tower, and all the ways to dealing with that. Aesthetically also, it's the way you cut the models when printing, just sort of slices in the middle of the building. It's kind of bizarre. However, I think typologically and aesthetically those are from the outside very important moments in your design. It just seems it's undercooked in relationship to the whole tower.

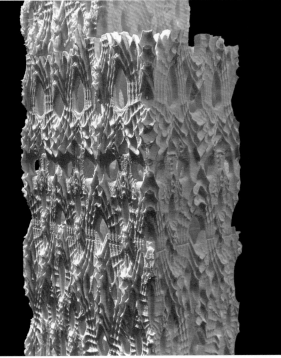

INVISIBLE TOWER

INVISIBLE TOWER IS DESIGNED TO BE THE HOME OF BIOTECH STARTUPS, A HUB WHERE BIOLOGICAL SCIENCES AND TECHNOLOGY CAN INTERMINGLE AND OVERLAP TO SPARK NEW DISCOVERIES AND INNOVATION. FEATURING LABORATORIES, BIO BANKS, AS WELL AS WORK AND EXHIBITION SPACES, THE TOWER SERVES A PIVOTAL ROLE IN CATALYZING BIOTECH AMBITIONS AND TRANSLATING THEM INTO REAL-WORLD INVESTMENT OPPORTUNITIES AND SPIN-OFFS SHROUDED IN A CORPORATE VEIL RENDERING IT INVISIBLE.

ALI TABATABAIE GHOMI, YUCHI WANG, MEARI KIM

JURY DISCUSSION

Cohen: Ultimately there is the matter of the theater. And I'm skeptical about the laboratories with such tiny floor plates. As far as performing in domestic ways, it starts to lose potential it becomes too ridiculous. It is not fun to think about things that are ridiculous, actually. As a child, thinking about things that are ridicules is fun because the child believes they are not ridiculous. There is a moment that is suspended in the game of being ridiculous. But when you are playing this game with adults it loses its interest pretty quickly—unless it is really funny in some really remarkable ways. But I don't think you are going for that. You are very serious about something that is ridiculous so I need a little bit more of an explanation. It's not quite entirely ridiculous but its verging on it. This is how this thing becomes critical not only in terms of how things work or do not work by a given footprint, but by what means we can understand their functions. So what is it about the logic of a Monsanto laboratory that can benefit from extreme verticalization? Is there some fiction or narrative that we can consider and integrate into the architectural expression? This one is interesting when you think about a theater underneath. Then, as a fiction it becomes believable. So, what is it about verticalizing laboratories? Performances are very special so you have to think about what types of performances can happen in these spaces. But as far as your showcase spaces, where some person is all alone and has their own executive office, you can have the whole floor be a single office space and just sit there all day with your laptop. There is no function at all other than just the idea of not being at a typical office. These are performing in a normal way and we have to think of a narrative for this. They could just be single floor suites.

Kolatan: The problem is that they are drawn like actual theaters rather than taking the concept of a theater and questioning whether this works in tower typology. This would necessarily lead to a different kind of plan and section of a theater because it is true that to see the miniature version of something that wants to be much larger is problematic. But this doesn't necessarily mean that the idea of the theater in this tower is completely meaningless.

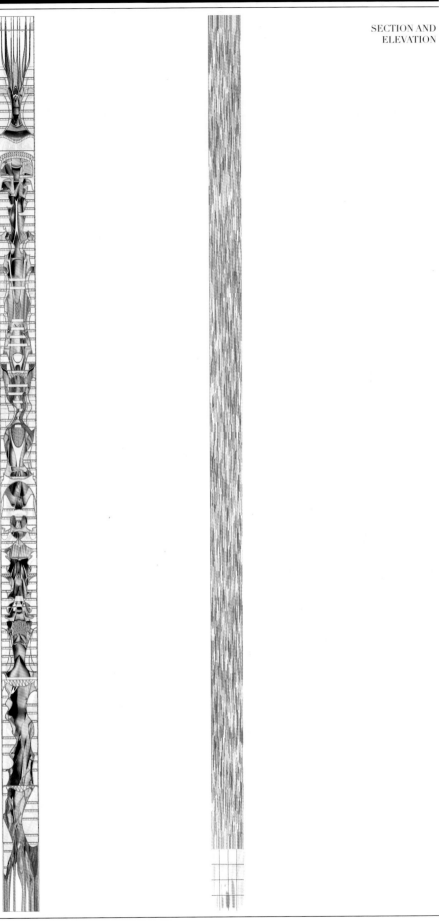

Cohen: The question is about how small the footprint is.

Douglis: The offices are interesting.

Jamelle: The lab is also not far away in terms of the offices we are looking at. Look at where labs are going now. They are no longer just on campuses. These are storage units. Storage units for people's DNA, for people's medical related-things. I am just talking about where technologies are taking different industries.

Soules: It would be good to see some plans that we get implementally broken into tiny bits. That is what we are doing. You are breaking the field that only performs as a lab in a large plate, a much larger than this and how it gets broken into unify. You going to do a diagram saying what would I do? what would they do to make a lab in such a tiny floor.

Douglis: How many square meters for each floor?

Cohen: It seems to me that being conservative, as opposed to pushing the boundaries of believability, is a positive attribute so far as this is an incredibly projective studio. Can you assign any program to this building and build it vertically, or do certain programs offer more opportunities to accommodate an affinity between a potential business model and architectural investigations that attempt to transform our notion of what a skyscraper is? This particular proposal brings in the a high degree of specificity in terms of what working in a lab is. It claims to do this in the plans and sections. The arguments would be that this lab has to offer an enormous amount of flexibility to be able to change the market, change new science, or whole series of things. So, it is fair to be cruel that this is much more

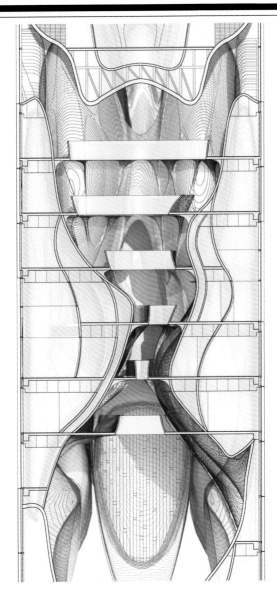

of a composition programmatically and the irony of this project is that they have chosen a facade that is all about being anonymous. In other words, it is almost what you would expect. There is absolutely no attempt to continue this on the inside. In other words, they could have taken the argument that, if you look at the plans and sections, they are more generic but also beautifully sculpted in terms of how they are managed, which doesn't look like anything in this studio and they perform pretty remarkably.

Soules: The irony in this project is that they chose a facade which has no intention continuing its qualities on the inside. And if you look at the plan and section, they are more generic. You can see how they manage it and it does not look like anything in the studio. I think the program of labs creates some problems for them that other projects don't have because they are more like residential or institutional buildings that are more about public accessibility. So this is a really interesting thing to discuss.

Jamelle: What if he explains a new typology of labs, like a whole new world for the pharma industry? If he describes it in these terms, the scale become less of a problem. You can think of the building as a large corporate campus with 18 buildings interconnected, including lab, training buildings, and so on. That's not what you guys thinking about, like a whole campus including two thousand people.

Rahim: The project was to have complete camouflage of its corporate identity. A firm like Monsanto is unwilling to be associated with the outer world. So the facade is different from the interior and the interior serves the function of gene banks and so on.

"THIS PARTICULAR PROPOSAL BRINGS IN THE COOPERATION AND A HIGH DEGREE OF SPECIFICITY IN TERMS OF ACCOMMODATING THE AFFINITY BETWEEN A POTENTIAL BUSINESS MODEL, ARCHITECTURAL INVESTIGATION AND AN ATTEMPT TO TRANSFORMING A TOWER TO THE NEW SKY SCRAPER."
PRESTON SCOTT COHEN

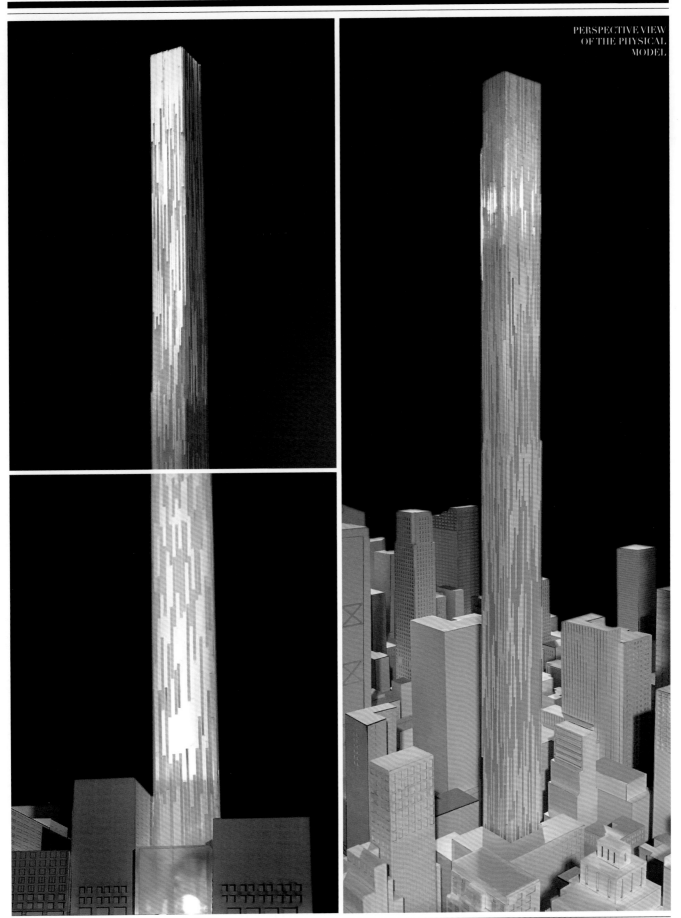

A NOVEL SOLUTION TO MOMA'S STORAGE PROBLEMS, STORAGE TOWER REPRESENTS A NEW PARADIGM IN ACCESSIBLE AND FUNCTIONAL ART STORAGE AND CURATION.THE TOWER WILL SERVE AS MOMA'S NEW STORAGE FACILITY WHILE ALSO OFFERING SPACES FOR DISPLAY AND RESEARCH.

LIANGQI SONG, YUNZHONGDA PENG, KYUHUN KIM

STORAGE TOWER

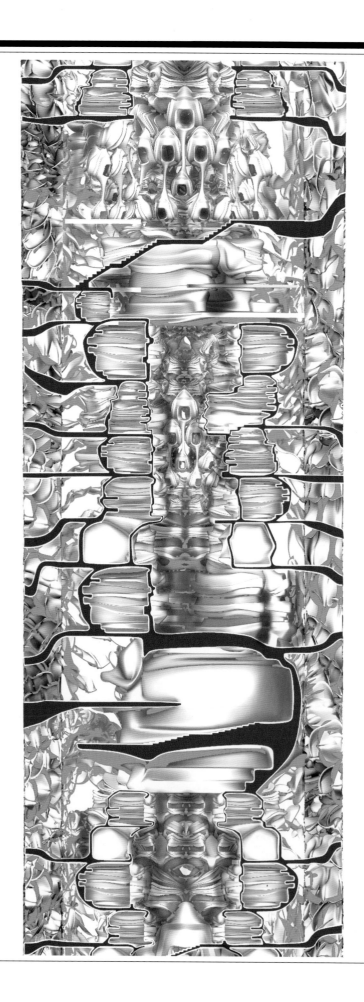

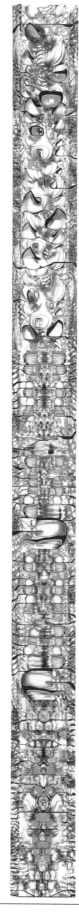

DETAILED SECTION
DRAWING

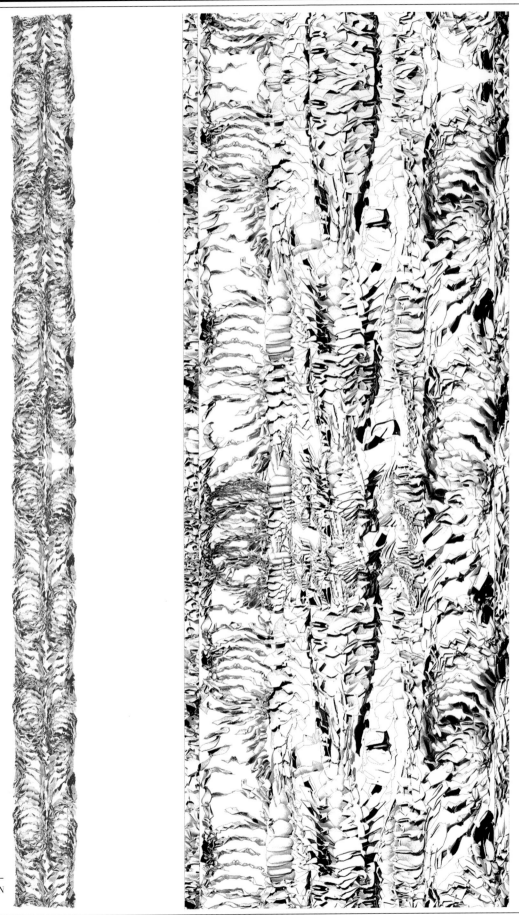

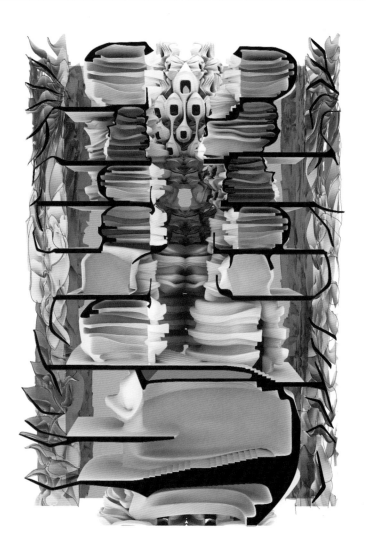

Jamelle: It is like a metamorphic canyon in nature. And that could be an idea for storage. In terms of a metamorphic rock, this means it has layers. If you have layers and layers of materials you could be showing layers of art and layers in which storage can happen. In history, you look at a timeline, layers represent time and together they comprise a timeline. Storage related to time or the way it is organized. This section is a good place to start. You have control over what the storage can be in terms of packing, a new way of packing and layering aspects together. You've explored different packing conditions.

Soules: The rendering is really exciting, however your section has some fascinating moments that are somewhat at odds with the plans. There is this intestinal orifice. There is also this black hole under the stage, as if you did not have enough money. It is a laboratory for competitions revolving around art and the procurement of art. You're going to have to go a long way to make the storage workable. The voluptuousness and the experience of the colored form is amazing. It is about movement, light devoured by the intensity of the architecture, which is really exciting.

Verebes: This would've been a great opportunity to resist the temptation to have over-articulation and lots and lots of small spaces on the interior, to have it be the biggest decorated shed we've ever seen in the history of architecture. That would have brought a counterargument to it and pushed back on some of the issues promoted in the studio, a totalized environment and a super articulated one, which doesn't mean small spaces. That could have been an opportunity to see that. That's the difference between the façade and the interior. The façade is nicely articulated and has a balance of scale that from any distance you can grasp the articulation. It's from here that the section is over-articulated but when you zoom in, it does not look like enough articulation. The proximity of that is over-simplified formally. And so the programming of this could have been far more engaging with the discourse in terms of the generic versus the highly articulated. It's like a turducken.

"THE VOLUPTUOUSNESS
AND THE EXPERIENCE
OF THE COLORED
FORM GENERATE THE
INTESTINAL MOVEMENT—
IT IS FASCINATING TO SEE
THE LIGHTS DEVOURED
BY THE INTENSITY OF THIS
ARCHITECTURE."
MATTHEW SOULES

GARMENT TOWER

GARMENT TOWER IS DEFINED BY ITS SINGULAR AESTHETIC AND LARGE-SCALE PUBLIC SPACE..JUST OFF CENTRAL PARK, THIS TOWER STANDS OUT FROM ITS CONTEXT WITH ITS UNIQUE FAÇADE DESIGN AND GENEROUS PUBLIC SPACE.

GE YANG, YUNLONG ZHANG, HAO FU

DETAILED VIEW
OF THE FACADE

JURY DISCUSSION

Rahim: This is a replacement for Madison Square Garden. But instead of theatric or sporting events, it is for corporate
              events. Instead of watching sports, for example, you are watching the city itself.

Dubbeldam: I think the moment on the facade is really clarifying. I like the insert which is really nice. It has different levels
              or different scales. It intensely defends the different kinds of space and makes the boundary very clear. The
              smaller scales really intensify the use of the space. And sometimes the space is compressed and then you can
              step out and feel the apex of the space. And this is where it is really worth it.

Verebes: It's really a good idea to have these pleated elements with the vertical straight lines at the same time. The
              contrast you make is the most amazing part in you project.

Massey: I think one of the most amazing things about your tower is that it is the first of all the towers, other than this
              Dolce & Gabbana moment, where the interior really distends and permeates from the interior to the exterior
              in a very strategic way in a few moments. I don't know why they happen when they happen but having that
              contrast is amazing, rather than the façade being one thing and the interior being another thing. This is one of

DETAILED ELEVATION DRAWING

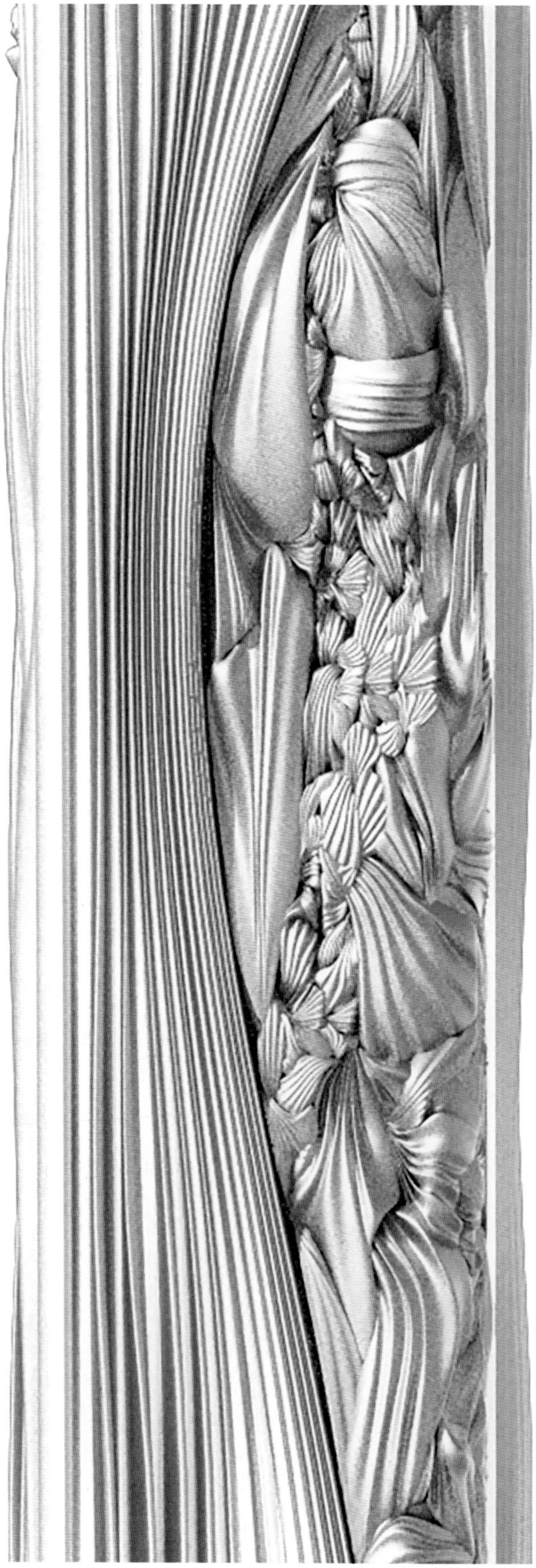

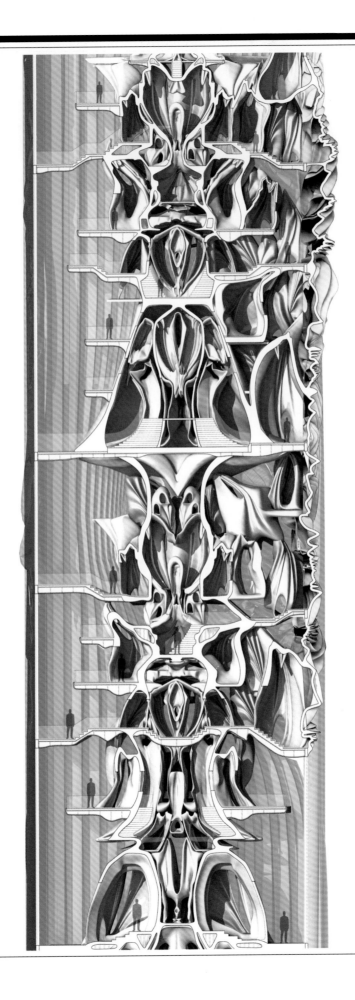

"THE EXTREME JUXTAPOSITIONS AND HETEROGENEITY BETWEEN TWO RADICALLY DIFFERENT TYPES OF EXPRESSIONS MAKES IT A REALLY AMAZING TYPE OF CONTEMPORARY PROJECT. THE FAÇADE OPENS UP TO THE INTERIOR— SIMPLE BUT ELEGANT."
JONATHAN MASSEY

those moments when you get, in an urban sense, that the building is really about extreme juxtapositions and the heterogeneity between two radically different types of expressions and that in some ways this is a really amazing contemporary project, and hard to pull off without it seeming like a collage. The fact that it separates and makes the pleats on the façade pull away means that it is not at all a collage from one type of expression to another but more about the façade opening up to the interior. It's simple yet elegant.

Soules: There is a richness we haven't seen a lot of in this reciprocal relationship. Part of me is sort of uncomfortable with it because it seems to be binary. It's not a collage but it is still a strong binary that seems to carry too much of a normative notion of skin and interior. This vector of the normative tower component lives on, so I wonder how the two can implicate each other more in an intensified symbiotic relationship as opposed to the veil making room. I'm curious as to how integrated it gets into the layers.

Kolatan: The exterior and interior have an interesting relationship. I'm not sure what happens differently in the different parts, but I do think the contrast is amazing. Rather than the interior being one thing and the façade another, like in many other projects, in yours they have a close relationship. The building is really about an extreme position in New York. It is about two definitively different expressions. I think, to some degree, it is really an amazing concrete project. You have two parts on the façade and the pleated part actually makes the section. The interior is very open to outside. I like it.

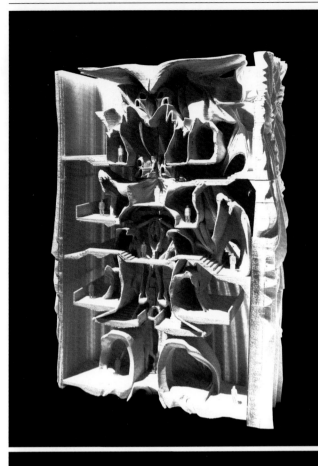

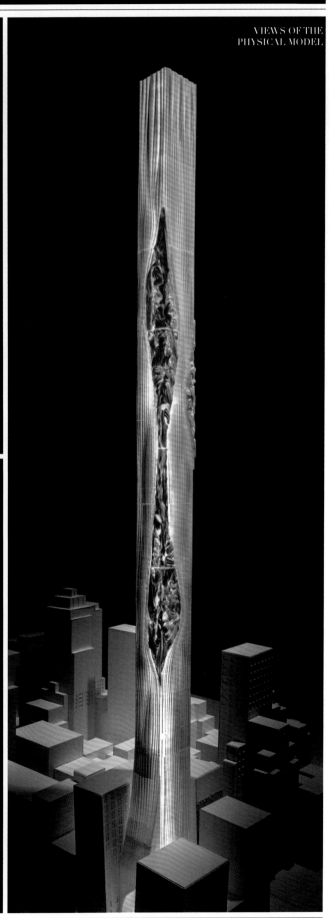

STUDIO CULTURE

STUDIO
TRIP IN NY

1. TOUR AT GOLDMAN SACHS HEADQUATERS IN NEW YORK
2. LUNCHTIME CRITIQUES
3. CONVERSATION BETWEEN STUDENTS AND INSTRUCTORS AFTER DINNER
4. STUDENT DINNER

1. STUDIO PHOTO AT GOLDMAN SACHS AGAINST THE BACK-DROP OF WORLD TRADE CENTER

2. LECTURE BY MARTHA KELLEY

3. STUDIO PHOTO AT GOLDMAN SACHS LOBBY

4. LECTURE BY PATRIK SCHUMACHER AT ARUP NEW YORK

DIGITAL
PRODUCTION

1	
2	
3	4

1. ONE VENTURE CAPITAL: GROUP DISCUSSION

2. ONE MILLION TOWER: MODELING PARTS WITH TEAMMATES

3. VERTICAL MAUSOLEUM: DIGITAL MODELING

4. GARMENT TOWER: DRAWING AND DISCUSSION

MIDREVIEW

1. REVIEW IN LOWER GELLERY
2. INSTRUCTORS AND MIDREVIEW JURORS
3. ONE VENTURE CAPITAL: PRESENTIATION
4. JURORS: (FROM LEFT TO RIGHT) ALI RAHIM, NICHOLAS KLEIN, DAN WOOD

1. ORNAMENT TOWER:
   EMBEDDING PARTS
2. NESTED MORPH:
   ASSEMBLING COMPONENTS
3. GARMENT TOWER:
   LAYERED FACADE
4. VERTICAL MAUSOLEUM:
   PRINTED PARTS

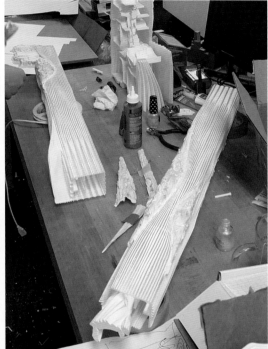

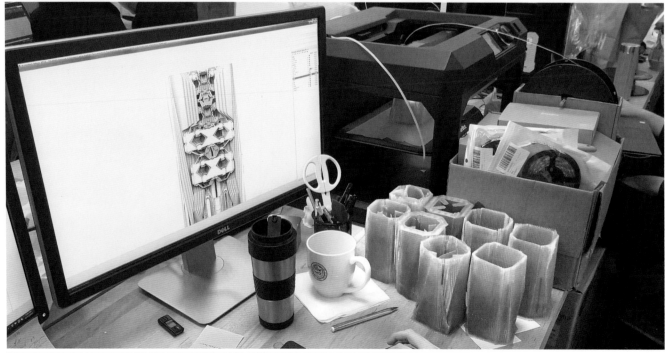

MODEL
PRODUCTION

1. NESTED MORPH:
   FACADE DETAIL
2. ONE MILLION TOWER:
   BUILDING TOWER
3. INVISIBLE TOWER:
   EXPLODED DETAILED MODEL
4. ORNAMENT TOWER:
   LAYERED FACADE

DESIGN
STUDIO

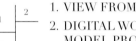

1. VIEW FROM MEETING ROOM
2. DIGITAL WORK AND PHYSICAL MODEL PRODUCTION
3. ALL 3D PRINTERS RUNNING FOR PRODUCTION
4. PHYSICAL MODEL OF THE CITY OF NEW YORK

1. NESTED MORPH AND ONE MILLION TOWER BEFORE THE FINAL REVIEW
2. MOVING TOWARDS EXHIBITION HALL
3. CARRYING OUT SITE MODEL FROM STUDIO SPACE
4. SITE MODELS SET IN THE FINAL REVIEW SPACE

```
    ┌───┬───
  1 │ 2 │
    │   ├───
    │ 3 │
    └───┴───
      4
```

FINAL REVIEW

1
2

1. PHYSICAL MODELS OF
ALL THE PROJECTS
EXIHIBITED IN
THE FINAL REVIEW
GALLERY

2. JURORS:
(FROM LEFT TO RIGHT)
ALI RAHIM(INSTRUCTOR),
HINA JAMELLE,
PRESTON SCOTT COHEN,
EVAN DOUGLIS,
TOM VEREBES,
MATTHEW SOULES,
JONATHAN MASSEY

JURY
DISCUSSION

TOP: JURORS:
PRESTON SCOTT COHEN, JONATHAN MASSEY

MIDDLE: JURORS: (FROM LEFT TO RIGHT)
HINA JAMELLE, FERDA KOLATAN, MATTHEW
SOULES, PRESTON SCOTT COHEN, EVAN
DOUGLIS, TOM VEREBES

BOTTOM: STUDIO INSTRUCTORS:
EZIO BLASETTI, ROBERT NEUMAYR,
ALI RAHIM, NATHAN HUME
JURORS: MATTHEW SOULES, BOŠTJAN
VUGA, WINKA DUBBELDAM

Faculty

Instructors

Ali Rahim is a Full Professor at the University of Pennsylvania School of Design where he directs the Advanced Architecture Design Program. He has served as the Studio Zaha Hadid Visiting Professor at the University of Applied Arts in Vienna, as the Louis I. Kahn Visiting Professor at Yale University, and as a Visiting Architecture Professor at Harvard University and SCI-Arc.

He is also Director of Contemporary Architecture Practice with Hina Jamelle in SoHo, New York City, and Shanghai, China. The firm is known for its award-winning and futuristic work that uses digital techniques for the design and manufacturing of architecture. Their portfolio includes a wide range and scale of work from furniture to master plans. His projects have been exhibited extensively, at such locations as the Museum of Modern Art (New York), the Serpentine Gallery (London), and the Tel Aviv Museum of Art. He has received many awards for his work including 50 under 50, Architectural Record Design Vanguard, Architectural Record Interiors, Architectural Record Products, Phaidon Press Interiors, and FEIDAD, to name a few. His work has been published in over 200 domestic and international magazines, journals, and newspapers. His authored publications include *Catalytic Formations: Architecture and Digital Design* (2012), published by the China Building Press, Beijing; *Catalytic Formations: Architecture and Digital Design* (2006), published by Routledge, London; *Turbulence* (2011), published by Norten and Company, New York; and three edited issues of *Architectural Design, Elegance* (2007), co-edited with Hina Jamelle, *Contemporary Techniques in Architecture* (2002), and *Contemporary Processes in Architecture* (2000).

Ali Rahim
Professor of Architecture
Director of MSD-AAD

Robert Neumayr is a Lecturer at University of Pennsylvania School of Design and an assistant professor in Kazuyo Seijma's design studio at the University of Applied Arts in Vienna. He has taught and lectured in Austria and internationally, among others working as an assistant professor with Patrik Schumacher in the Department for Experimental Architecture at the University of Innsbruck (AT) and as assistant professor with Zaha Hadid at the Institute of Architecture at the University of Applied Arts in Vienna from 2008 to 2015.

He is co-founder and director of unsquare.org in Vienna, which brings together academia, design research and professional practice.

His research focuses on responsive architecture, parametric urbanism, algorithmic design, and contemporary digital design practice. His research and projects have been published and exhibited internationally, most notably at *Latent Utopias* (Graz, 2002) and the *Beijing Biennale* (Beijing, 2004), and been awarded the Bronze Medal at the *Miami Biennale* 2003.

He is currently working on his PhD on Agent Based Parametric Semiology.

Robert Neumayr
Lecturer

Nathan Hume is a partner at Hume Coover Studio with Abigail Hume. Hume Coover Studio strives to engage popular culture and contemporary architectural form through built and speculative projects, with an emphasis on experimenting with the organization of space through complex geometry, innovative materials, and counter-intuitive planning. Nathan received his Masters of Architecture from the Yale University School of Architecture. Nathan and Abigail's work and writings have been published in the *New York Times*, *Wired*, *Metropolis*, *Tarp*, and *Project* and exhibited at the Yale University School of Architecture, the New York Center for Architecture and the Museum of Modern Art. Abigail and Nathan are also co-creators and editors of suckerPUNCHdaily.com a website that reviews the work of contemporary artists, architects, and designers who offer the stunningly unexpected and beautiful. Through suckerPUNCH they mounted the exhibition *Fresh Punches* at the Land of Tomorrow gallery and published the accompanying book.

Nathan Hume
Lecturer

Ezio Blasetti is a designer who earned a Master of Science in advanced architectural design from Columbia University after having previously studied in Athens and Paris. In 2009 he co-founded ahylo, a design, research and construction practice as well as "apomechanes," an annual intensive summer studio on algorithmic processes and fabrication. Founder of algorithmicdesign.net, Ezio is 1/3 of Serge Studio and his recent collaborations include biothing, acconci studio, and a|Um studio. His recent work at Acconci Studio has received awards in international competitions – 2008 Annual Design Review I.D. / Perm Museum XXI / Kravi Hora Sculpture Park. He has taught generative design studios and seminars by means of computational geometry at Pratt Institute, the Architectural Association, Rensselaer Polytechnic Institute, and Columbia University. He is a registered architect in Greece, where in 2004 he co-founded otn studio, a young design-build practice, and completed several projects. His work has been exhibited and published internationally and is part of the permanent collection of the Centre Pompidou (with biothing).

Ezio Blasetti
Lecturer

Teaching Assistants

Maru Chung
Lois S. K. Suh
Kristy Kimball
Tong Qi

Authors

See Faculty

Ali Rahim
Professor of Architecture
Director of MSD-AAD
University of Pennsylvania

See Faculty

Robert Neumayr
Lecturer
University of Pennsylvania

Matthew Soules is an Assistant Professor at the University of British Columbia and the director of Matthew Soules Architecture. His firm has received numerous awards including the Architectural Institute of British Columbia's Emerging Firm (2010) and Special Jury Awards in 2010 and 2015 respectively, an Architizer A+ Award in the Cultural Pavilions Category in 2015 and a selection by Twenty + Change in 2011.

Matthew Soules
Assistant Professor
The University of
British Columbia

Tom Verebes is the founder and Creative Director of OCEAN.CN, and co-founder of OCEAN, and company Director of OCEAN UK Design Ltd. He has served as Associate Dean in the Faculty of Architecture and is currently Associate Professor in the Department of Architecture at the University of Hong Kong. Formerly Co-Director of the AA Design Research Lab at the Architectural Association in London; and current Director of the AA Shanghai Visiting School.

Tom Verebes
Lecturer
University of Pennsylvania

Preston Scott Cohen is the Chair of the Department of Architecture and the Gerald M. McCue Professor of Architecture at Harvard University Graduate School of Design. He is the author of Contested Symmetries (Princeton Architectural Press, 2001) and numerous theoretical and historical essays on architecture. He has held faculty positions at Princeton, RISD, and Ohio State University.

Preston Scott Cohen
Chair
Gerald M. McCue Professor
Harvard University

Evan Douglis is the principal of Evan Douglis Studio LLC; an internationally renowned interdisciplinary design firm. The firm's unique cutting edge research into computer-aided digital design and fabrication technology as applied to a range of diverse gallery installations, product designs, commercial and residential projects, urban redevelopment schemes and prefabricated modular building components has elicited international acclaim.

Evan Douglis
Dean | Professor
Rensselaer Polytechnic Institute

Brian DeLuna currently has an atelier in New York and is a lecturer at Rensselaer Polytechnic Institute. Previous teaching experience includes teaching as an Assistant Professor at the Angewandte_University of Applied Arts in Vienna, The New Jersey Institute of Technology and at Princeton University; assistant to Hani Rashid.

Brian DeLuna
Lecturer
Rensselaer Polytechnic Institute

Winka Dubbeldam is a seasoned academic and design leader, serving as Chair and Professor of Graduate Architecture at PennDesign, where she has has gathered an international network of innovative research and design professionals. Previously, Professor Dubbeldam oversaw the Post-Professional Degree program providing students with innovative design skills, cutting edge theoretical and technological knowledge.

Winka Dubbeldam
Chair
Professor of Architecture
University of Pennsylvania

Joshua Freese is a full-time lecturer in the Department of Architecture at the University of Pennsylvania School of Design. He is the founder of Freese LLC/Freese Design Studio in Philadelphia, PA. He has previously worked for and with !Melk, ISA, HWKN, UN Studio and OMA. Joshua's work explores pattern making and parametric design, ranging from generative computational design to BIM and fabrication strategies and solutions.

Joshua Freese
Lecturer
University of Pennsylvania

Hina Jamelle is an Architect and Director at Contemporary Architecture Practice in Shanghai and New York. Active in education, Hina teaches graduate design studios atthe University of Penssylvania and the Pratt Institute. Her work with CAP has been exhibited at MOMA, the Serpentine Gallery in London, amongst others. Her work has been published in news and scholarly organizations from The New York Times, to Architectural Design and Spa-De in Japan.

Hina Jamelle
Senior Lecturer
Director of Urban Housing
University of Pennsylvania

Jurors and Critics through the Year

Ferda Kolatan is an Associate Professor of Practice at PennDesign and the founding director of su11 in New York City. He as lectured widely and taught design studios as well as theory and fabrication seminars at Columbia University, Cornell University, Rensselaer Polytechnic Institute, University of British Columbia, California College of the Arts, Washington University, Pratt Institute, and the RWTH Aachen.

Ferda Kolatan
Associate Professor
of Practice
University of Pennsylvania

Nicholas Klein is a screenwriter and film producer. His writings range across drama, thriller, and mestery, and he received numerous international awards including 2000 Jury Prize at Berlin Film Festival for The Million Dollar Hotel(2000). The End of Violence(1997) was also praised by critics for its cinematography and entered into the 1997 Cannes Film Festival, and The Venice Project(1999) was nominated for Golden Lion at Venice Film Festical in 1999.

Nicholas Klein
Screenwriter

Jonathan Massey is Dean of Architecture at the California College of the Arts. Previously he was the Meredith Professor for Teaching Excellence at Syracuse University, where he also chaired the Bachelor of Architecture program and the University Senate. As co-founder of the Transdisciplinary Media Studio and the Aggregate Architectural History Collaborative, he has published in many journals and essay collections, including the jointly edited volume Governing by Design.

Jonathan Massey
Dean
Professor of Architecture
California Colledge of the Arts

Andrew Saunders Architecture+Design is an internationally published, award winning architecture, design and research practice committed to the tailoring of innovative digital methodologies to provoke novel exchange and reassessment of the broader cultural context. The practice innovates at a number of scales ranging from product design, residential design, to large-scale civic and cultural institutional design.

Andrew Saunders
Associate Professor
University of Pennsylvania

See Authors.

Matthew Soules
Assistant Professor
The University of
British Columbia

See Authors

Tom Verebes
Lecturer
University of Pennsylvania

Boštjan Vuga is a founder of SADAR+VUGA architectural office along with Jurij Sadar. He has taught at the Berlage Institute Rotterdam, the IAAC Barcelona, the Faculty of Architecture Ljubljana, TU Berlin and MSA Muenster, and was a visiting critic at AA London, the Bauhaus Kolleg in Dessau, the ETH in Zürich, Leopold-Franzens-Univeristaet Innsbruck, EIA Ecole D'ingenieurs et d'architectes Fribourg, the Academy of Visual Arts Vienna among others.

Boštjan Vuga
President of MAO Museum
Architecture and Design
Slovenia

Danielle Willems is a partner at the firm Maeta Design LLC, where she progressively merges several disciplines such as industrial design, fashion design, motiongraphics and film into her architectural design methodologies. Since 2008, Danielle has taught at Rensselaer Polytechnic Institute, Cooper Union, Columbia University and is currently a lecturer at University of Pennsylvania and an assistant professor at Pratt Institute.

Danielle Willems
Lecturer
University of Pennsylvania

Dan Wood leads international projects for WORK. ac ranging from masterplans to buildings across the United States as well as in Asia, Africa, and Europe. Wood is a Principal at WORK ARCHITECTURE COMPANY, which he founded in 2003 with Amale Andraos. Since its beginnings, their office has developed a body of projects aimed at rethinking accepted norms, to both envision and realize alternative possibilities for the built environment.

Dan Wood
Lecturer
University of Pennsylvania

SPEEDTRADER

Andres Daniel Cely
Tianyi Sun
Yuhan Bian

SKYHOUSE

Boqun Huai
Yue Peng
Hewen Jiang

HEPHAESTUS

Shuoqi Xiong
Kai Tang
Jia Lyu

VERSACE TOWER

Xi Chen
Fangjie Guo
Yijia Wang

KALEIDOSCOPE TOWER

Xiaoyu Ma
Jieping Wan
Kaikang Shen

NESTED MORPH

Siyang Lv
Can Wang
Yuchen Zhao
Sookwan Ahn

ONE MILLION TOWER

Jiangbao Zhong
Mengyue Wu
Xiaonan Chen

Angeliki Tzifa
Ke Liu
Dongliang Li

THE ABYSS

Xuechuan Qin
Ce Li
Jingyi Sun

PLOUTO

Bosung Jeon
Carrie Rose Frattali
Xiaoyu Zhao

VERTICAL MAUSOLEUM

Taeseo Park
Musab Mohammad
Xiaoyi Gao

ONE VENTURE CAPITAL

Ali Tabatabaie Ghomi
Yuchi Wang
Meari Kim

INVISIBLE TOWER

Liangqi Song
Yunzhongda Peng
Kyuhun Kim

STORAGE TOWER

Ge Yang
Yunlong Zhang
Hao Fu

GARMENT TOWER
2017 EVOLO COMPETITION HONORABLE MENTION

Acknowledgements

This book was made possible by funding from the University of Pennsylvania School of Design and Department of Architecture. I would like to personally thank Dean Frederick Steiner for his support.

I would also like to thank the Master of Science in Design, Advanced Architectural Design students at the University of Pennsylvania who worked diligently to conceptualize and develop their work within the studio. My fellow faculty members Robert Neumayer, Nathan Hume, and Ezio Blasetti contributed greatly through our many discussions and their teaching. Lois Suh, Maru Chung, Kristy Kimball, and Tong Qi contributed in their roles as teaching assistants. Ezio Blasetti and Danielle Willems started the students off very well with a short class in digital techniques that inspired and elevated the design acumen of the students. Finally I would like to thank all of the participants who contributed to the discussions during the reviews: Preston Scott Cohen, Evan Douglis, Winka Dubbeldam, Joshua Freese, Hina Jamelle, Ferda Kolatan, Nicholas Klein, Jonathan Massey, Andrew Saunders, Matthew Soules, Tom Verebes, Boštjan Vuga, Danielle Willems, and Dan Wood.

A special thanks to ARUP New York, Goldman Sachs New York and Zaha Hadid Architects. Gillian Blake of ARUP lectured brilliantly on the infrastructure of the City of New York and allowed ARUP's use of their space at 77 Water Street for Penn activities including her lecture and dinner. Martha Kelley of Goldman Sachs lectured at 200 West Street and described private sector funded projects in great detail that are developed by Goldman Sachs in New York City. Patrik Schumacher spoke about the differences in architecture practice during the early 2000's and today articulating his vision for incorporating difference into the process and work of architecture. He concluded with his thoughts on asset architecture as he is in the midst of designing 520 W. 28th Street in the Chelsea district of Manhattan. This discussion elevated the discourse within the time with the students but also elevated the work of the students considerably. All three of these lecture experiences were invaluable in the development of the criticality in thought and understanding of development of asset architecture in New York City.

Lastly, Ryosuke Imaeda, a graduated of the MSD, Advanced Architectural Design program has been heroic in his work on *Asset Architecture 3*. I would also like to thank Guy Horton for his relentless work on editing the texts in this volume.

Ali Rahim
Professor of Architecture and Director, MSD-Advanced Architectural Design, University of Pennsylvania

PUBLISHERS OF ARCHITECTURE, ART, AND DESIGN
GORDON GOFF: PUBLISHER

WWW.OROEDITIONS.COM
INFO@OROEDITIONS.COM

PUBLISHED BY ORO EDITIONS

GRAPHIC DESIGN: RYOSUKE IMAEDA
TRANSCRIPTION OF JURY COMMENTS: RYOSUKE IMAEDA, KRISTY KIMBALL
PROJECT COORDINATOR: KIRBY ANDERSON

10 9 8 7 6 5 4 3 2 1 FIRST EDITION

LIBRARY OF CONGRESS DATA AVAILABLE UPON REQUEST. WORLD RIGHTS: AVAILABLE

ISBN:978-1-940743-73-8

COLOR SEPARATIONS AND PRINTING: ORO GROUP LTD.
PRINTED IN CHINA.

INTERNATIONAL DISTRIBUTION: WWW.OROEDITIONS.COM/DISTRIBUTION

ORO EDITIONS MAKES A CONTINUOUS EFFORT TO MINIMIZE THE OVERALL CARBON FOOTPRINT OF ITS PUBLICATIONS.
AS PART OF THIS GOAL, ORO EDITIONS, IN ASSOCIATION WITH GLOBAL RELEAF, ARRANGES TO PLANT TREES TO REPLACE
THOSE USED IN THE MANUFACTURING OF THE PAPER PRODUCED FOR ITS BOOKS. GLOBAL RELEAF IS AN INTERNATIONAL
CAMPAIGN RUN BY AMERICAN FORESTS, ONE OF THE WORLD'S OLDEST NONPROFIT CONSERVATION ORGANIZATIONS.
GLOBAL RELEAF IS AMERICAN FORESTS' EDUCATION AND ACTION PROGRAM THAT HELPS INDIVIDUALS, ORGANIZATIONS,
AGENCIES, AND CORPORATIONS IMPROVE THE LOCAL AND GLOBAL ENVIRONMENT BY PLANTING AND CARING FOR TREES.

FRONT COVER IMAGE: VERTICAL MAUSOLEUM

Bosung Jeon, Carrie Rose Frattali, Xiaoyu Zhao